Miami Beach
100 Years of Making Waves
by
Charles J. Kropke and Eleanor Goldstein
Joe Davis, Artist

2015

Preface

Slowly, steadily, inexorably, inevitably; a barrier island off of the Southeast Coast of the Florida Peninsula was transformed from a sandbar to a thriving, bustling city, which came to be known as Miami Beach.

First came Native Americans, about fifteen thousand years ago, then came the explorers, about five hundred years ago, then came the pioneers, then came the settlers, then came the developers, then came the tourists, then came the residents to create permanent homes.

Alligators, snakes, bobcats, bear, raccoons; lost their habitat to intrepid humans who changed the swamp to suit their needs. The swamp gave way to sidewalks. The mangroves gave way to man-made structures.

Well; actually, it wasn't so slow. It took only a hundred years for Miami Beach to be transformed from a village of fewer than 100 people to a city of about 90,000 with vacation months soaring to more than twice that number.

With a population of around 100 people, the Town of Miami Beach was incorporated with 33 registered voters, who met on March 26, 1915 in the Ocean Beach Realty offices. They selected a mayor and aldermen and never looked back as they created a paradise to lure people from northern states. On May 21, 1917, with a population of about 200, the town of Miami Beach became a city by an act of the Florida Legislature.

Charles J. Kropke relates the history of these one hundred years by chronicling the stories of iconic establishments in Miami Beach. Many of the most familiar locations have interesting, little-known facts which make the history come alive. It is real; often fascinating, eccentric, people who Charles tells us about, with knowledge that comes from extensive research and many personal interviews.

Miami Beach has undergone the highest of highs and the lowest of lows. It has some of the wealthiest residents in the world and has sheltered some of the poorest. It has some of the safest neighborhoods, guarded with gates. In the 1980s and 1990s, it was one of the most crime-ridden cities in the nation.

Travel with Charles through a hundred years of Miami Beach history. It's a great journey you will never forget.

Miami Beach
100 Years of Making Waves

Beginnings — page 4

South Beach — page 16

South of Fifth — page 17
  Government Cut
  Browns Hotel
  Joe's Stone Crab
  Tap Tap Haitian Restaurant
  Jewish Museum of Florida-FIU

Ocean Drive — page 38
  Versace Mansion-Casa Casuarina
  Lummus Park
  Art Deco
  Wolfsonian-FIU
  Mango's Tropical Cafe
  Beach Patrol - Lifeguard Stations

Española Way — page 64
Venetian Isles — page 68
Lincoln Road — page 69
  Miami Beach Convention Center
  Loews / St. Moritz
  Holocaust Memorial
  New World Symphony
  Miami City Ballet

Mid Beach — page 88
  Fontainebleau and Eden Roc Hotels
  41st Street / Arthur Godfrey Road
  Normandy Isle Vendome Fountain
  LaGorce Island

North Beach — page 102
  Little Buenos Aires
  Mid Century Modern Architecture (MIMO)
  North Shore Open Space Park

Interviews — page 109
Bibliography — page 110
Biographies — page 111
Credits — page 112

Beginnings

Winter is generally cold, dreary and long in most of the United States. Once the leaves have abandoned the limbs and the autumn colors have subsided, gray skies take over and it can be many months until the arrival of spring when nature awakens the buds and the birds return and warm, pleasant weather lifts the spirits of the winter-weary residents.

By the late 1800s, NewYork City, Philadelphia, Chicago, Detroit, Indianapolis and Boston had populations in the millions. These Northern cities were the perfect target for the land boom that was created in South Florida in the early 1900s. It was great to learn that there was a tropical paradise within reach that could help alleviate the boredom and misery of the seemingly endless winter.

Miami Beach was incorporated as a town, on May 26, 1915 with a population of about one hundred people. The City of Miami was a small village, of about 25,000 people at that time. In the 1920s, Miami Beach experienced unprecedented growth.

Several events in history conspired to enable this to happen; the expansion of the railroad, the production of cheap cars, the building of national highways, and the development of a large middle-class. A cast of formidable, courageous, adventurous, creative, eccentric people emerged to transform the land of alligators, crocodiles, rabbits, rats and swarms of mosquitoes into a paradise for the super-rich and the middle-class.

Miami Beach is a long, narrow peninsula nestled between Biscayne Bay and the Atlantic Ocean. Its modern history dates back to the early 1900s, although early settlers from the City of Miami had been going to the beach since the 1880s when the first plantation was carved from the wilderness on the Miami River. It became a popular activity to row across the bay to the Miami Beach peninsula, then trek across the swamp to enjoy the sandy beach and the blue, often green, waters of the Atlantic Ocean.

In 1870, Henry Lum and his son, Charles, when sailing north from Key West, viewed the sandy coast of what would become Miami Beach and saw some coconut trees growing. This inspired them to believe that they could develop a coconut plantation. It took them twelve years, and they bought about 100 miles of land from Cape Florida to north of Jupiter, paying between 75 cents and $1.25 an acre. Several men were involved with the early purchase of land in the 1800s, but it is Lum who is credited with trying to establish the first business, a coconut plantation. Lum and his associates hired 25 men, purchased some old lifeboats from the government, picked up tens of thousands of coconuts leaving about 40,000 on Miami Beach. Rabbits and rats loved the coconut sprouts and ate them all, so that the coconut plantation was a failure.

Charles Lum and his wife built the first house on Miami Beach on what is now 11th Street and Ocean Drive. They lived in this house for about three years, but it was a lonely life and very uncomfortable for much of the year with the mosquitoes and hot, humid weather. By 1890, they returned to New Jersey.

At the urging of Julia Tuttle, a Miami developer, considered the "mother" of Miami, Henry Flagler extended his Florida East Coast Railroad to Miami from Palm Beach. When central and northern Florida crops were devastated by a freeze, Tuttle, had a bouquet of orange blossoms sent to Flagler to show him that the climate in Miami was more adaptable for winter growth than was central or northern Florida. Tuttle gave Flagler the deed to some land to induce him to continue the rail-road to Miami. By 1896 Miami had its railroad. Soon a regular flow of tourists and settlers came to Miami.

In 1904 a two story pavilion was built on the beach where people could seek shade and rent swimming suits for 25 cents. An elevated boardwalk was built from the pier to the pavilion. Ferries began to ply the Biscayne Bay waters to the beach from the City of Miami on a regular schedule.

A number of adventurers were investing and settling in Miami Beach during the 1880's and 1890's. John Collins was one of these men. Collins was a wealthy man from New Jersey who had invested $5,000 in the coconut plantation that Lum had tried to cultivate. He was an expert in the cultivation of fruit. Although the coconut plantation was a failure, Collins was intrigued by the possibility of the stretch of land along the coastline as a potential for growing other products.. He purchased five miles of coastline property and in 1907 planted avocado and mango trees, soon adding other fruits and vegetables such as potatoes, tomatoes and bananas. It was an arduous trip to bring his products to Miami to be sent up north by rail.

When his cash reserves began to dwindle, Collins sought assistance from his children and their spouses who were in successful businesses that he had previously helped them establish. He wanted them to help finance a canal from his property to the bay. When they came to visit, they were more impressed by the potential of the oceanfront property as a seaside resort. As a compromise, his children agreed to help finance a canal if Collins would commit to building a bridge across Biscayne Bay to Miami, which would then open the beach property to automobile traffic. Together they opened the Miami Beach Improvement Company, the first real estate company on the Beach.

In order to finance the building of the bridge, Collins and his son-in-law, Thomas Pancoast, turned to the Lummus brothers who were bankers in Miami. The Lummus brothers, recognizing the potential of beach front property after a bridge was built, purchased six hundred acres of land on the south tip of the island, and lent the money for the construction of the bridge. Collins and Pancoast, needed more financing when the bridge was about one-half mile from completion.

Carl Fisher was interested in the progress of the bridge as he also recognized the potential of the Beach. He was a millionaire from Indianapolis, who had made a fortune manufacturing headlights for cars, and founding the Indianapolis Speedway, among many other ventures. He agreed to financing the completion of the bridge, in exchange for two hundred acres of land from the ocean to the bay. He purchased an additional hundred acres from the Lummus brothers making him one of the largest land owners and a most influential man in Miami Beach.

The Collins Bridge was finished on June 12, 1913. It was a great event calling for a huge celebration. Pancoast led a caravan of cars across the bridge, which was the longest wooden bridge in the world. The land boom in Miami Beach escalated with development moving at a rapid pace with the Lummus brothers, Collins and Fisher promoting their holdings with great fanfare. In 1915, they combined efforts to create the Town of Miami Beach. The population was about 100 people with 33 registered voters.

The four early developers of Miami Beach had different objectives for their properties. Fisher wanted to cater to those with the greatest wealth. He planned yacht clubs, golf clubs, polo grounds and luxurious hotels for the very rich; Gentiles only. Collins and Pancoast wanted to create homes and hotels for the upper class, high income industrialists, also for Gentiles only. The Lummus brothers had a more modest approach to their development, hoping to attract middle class families with smaller sized lots. Their properties were restricted to blacks but available to other ethnic groups. The influence of these men is still significant in South Beach. Collins Avenue is the longest and most developed street on the beach; the Lummus brothers sold twenty acres of beachfront property which stretches from 5th to 15th streets for use as a park that defines South Beach today; and Fisher is credited with creating the infrastructure of streets and the planting of palms, banyan trees, hibiscus and bougainvillea as well as building hotels and providing sporting facilities.

Carl Fisher is considered the "father" of Miami Beach. He is commonly referred to by either of two words; "crazy" or "genius." He was born in Indiana in 1874. He had a severe astigmatism, so that he was handicapped at school and left formal learning when he was twelve. Abandoned by his alcoholic father, Carl started to work at an early age. When he was seventeen, he opened a bicycle shop with his two brothers. His nature was that of a dare-devil and promoter. He became a professional racing cyclist and performed outrageous acts of daring and courage; such as riding a bike on a high wire raised between two tall buildings in town. He also built a huge bicycle, two stories high, which he rode around town. When the automobile first came to town, Fisher was the first person to buy one, and he became an auto racer. His interest in racing led him to eventually create the Indianapolis Speedway. When someone introduced to him, the idea of replacing kerosene with compressed gas for headlights, he invested and formed the Prest-O-Lite Company.

The development of the headlight was a great boon to Miami Beach because it enabled people to drive

at night. In 1909, Carl married 15 year old Jane Watts. In 1913 he sold Prest-O-Lite for $9 million, the equivalent of $210 million dollars today. With the popularity of the car, Fisher believed it necessary to build roads. He was behind the development of the Lincoln Highway and the Dixie Highway. At the end of the Dixie Highway, the new City of Miami was growing, and Fisher became involved with real estate in Miami Beach. The coming together of these four men, Fisher, Collins and the Lummus Brothers led to the development of Miami Beach.

Few places have undergone as many transitions as Miami Beach. It has gone from boom to bust to boom many times in its history of a hundred years. The 1920s were eventful years. On New Year's Eve of 1921, Fisher opened the Flamingo Hotel on 15th Street and the Bay. In order to lure tourists to the area, a great publicity campaign took place and the beach was advertised as a place where "summer spends the winter". Billboards were posted in northern cities displaying bathing beauties and the word "cheesecake" was created to describe the phenomenon of young women parading in scanty swimming suits on sandy shores dotted with palm trees. The real estate boom that ensued can hardly be imagined. Streets were packed with frenetic buyers; beds were rented by shifts to laborers and salesmen in the few hotels that were available.

By 1920, the permanent population of Miami Beach was 644. The City of Miami had a telephone directory which listed 80 phones for Miami Beach. By 1925, there were 56 hotels containing 4,000 rooms, and 178 apartment houses. The years between 1920 and 1925 were very prosperous. There were beautiful, uncluttered beaches, extravagant hotels, and lots of entertainment. A sense of general well-being prevailed. Then on Saturday morning, September 18, 1926 a category 5 hurricane struck with wind gusts reaching 150 miles an hour. People were stunned. There weren't any hurricane warnings at the time. Roofs were blown away, hotel lobbies and streets were covered with sand, furniture was strewn all over. It is estimated that several hundred people were killed; thousands were injured. The weather bureau said it may have been the worst storm to ever hit the U.S. The shock of the damage spread across the nation. Tourists stayed away and land sales dipped precipitously. Miami Beach lost its appeal.

Soon to follow, in 1929, was the Great Depression which ravished the fortunes of many people and created huge unemployment. While the Depression caused havoc throughout the nation, Miami Beach was not as badly affected because those who were employed craved a getaway from the bleakness of the North. Developers responded by building smaller, inexpensive hotels.

Architecture was influenced by a movement, first popularized in Paris, which later became known as "Art Deco". During the 1930's, almost 200 hotels and 500 apartment buildings were built in the "Deco" style. In 1930, the population of Miami Beach was 6500 rising to 28,000 by the end of the decade. Art Deco hotels were mainly built between 6th and 15th streets along Ocean Drive and several blocks to the west. The style

of Art Deco includes elaborate facades, futuristic spires, nautical themes and neon lighting. Rooms were available at $5.00 to $8.00 a day including breakfast. So, even during a depression, they were affordable for a middle class budget. While architects were influenced by the movement, the term "Art Deco" was not applied to this style of architecture until 1966.

In 1942, during World War II, Miami Beach became a military training ground and hotels were requisitioned for that purpose. Construction for civilian use was suspended when the military took over. It is estimated that half-a-million men and women went through training in Miami Beach. Many of these people returned to Miami Beach to live after the war was over. By 1950, the population had reached 46,300 people.

The population of the area south of Fifth Street was largely Jewish, many who had been workers in the factories of the northeast and could afford to live on retirement and social security benefits. The neighborhoods north of Fifth were largely restricted to all but Gentiles. A lively community was created, south of Fifth, including clubs and delis. A pier was built at the end of the beach; included was Minski's Burlesque. A dog racing track was built. The annual income of this population was one of the lowest in the nation, and as the residents aged, the area went into decline. By 1970, the median age in South Beach was 64. The area became know as "God's waiting room." As the years passed, many of the hotels built in the 1930s' went into decay and were not being maintained. Developers preferred to build larger hotels, to maximize their income, and were moving north on Collins Avenue.

In 1980, Fidel Castro allowed about 125,000 people to leave Cuba during the Mariel boatlift. Many came to South Beach and moved into the run-down hotels and apartments. Among the refugees were about 15,000 who were released from prisons and mental institutuions. Many of those people were hardened criminals. The Federal Government paid the rent for these people. At the same time the international drug trade flourished and South Beach became a haven for smugglers and users. The neighborhood became dangerous for the elderly and infirm. The homeless, criminals, and substance users were taking over. South Beach seemed utterly hopeless.

The area between 6th and 15th Streets in South Beach was saved by a group of dedicated preservationists. Barbara Capitman, a journalist focusing on industrial design, was familiar with South Beach, having visited twenty years earlier. Shocked and dismayed by the decay of the once beautiful buildings, she went into high gear and organized others who felt as she did. They formed a group known as the Miami Design Preservation League (MDPL). Capitman's personality enamored many and enraged others. She was known to attend meetings in a long black dress, known as the Robes of Justice, and tennis shoes waving her arms to make a point she was passionate about. It has been said that she sometimes was dressed by her friends, since she did not pay attention to such mundane matters. The battles that ensued were legendary. She gave speeches

and stood in front of threatened buildings. She was in poor health, but that never stopped her from fighting for her beloved buildings. She once feigned a heart attack, first alerting the press that she was making a speech, to gain attention to her cause. Her organization grew to a thousand members. Their first task was to survey the area and identify buildings worthy of preservation. They found over a thousand buildings fitting the qualifications. Due to these efforts, the Miami Beach Architectural District was included on the National Register of Historic Places in 1979.

While Barbara Capitman and the Miami Design Preservation League were dedicated to revitalizing the area between 15th and 5th Streets, South of 5th was in chaos. A most remarkable book, entitled **Sins of South Beach** written by a former City Commissioner, and three term-Mayor of Miami Beach, Alex Daoud, revealed the corruption, and violence that prevailed in Miami Beach, especially in South Beach. Daoud describes in great detail how he personally was seduced by the rampant corruption in the area. He began his career as an idealistic, young attorney, but soon fell into the lifestyle that dominated the area in which bribery was a common way of life. Murder was an everyday occurrence and the elderly and poor were terrorized by criminals and drug addicts. He began to drive along with the police at night to patrol the neighborhood and they formed a group known as the "Attitude Adjustment Committee", in which they took justice into their own hands. They rounded-up criminals, beat them up, took their pants and money and deposited them outside the limits of the City, generally on the boundary of the City of Miami. The jails in Miami were so crowded that they quickly released the prisoners.

Eventually, Mayor Daoud was indicted on 41 counts of criminal activity, mostly bribery charges. He was acquitted on all but one. He could have gone to prison for life, but he co-operated with the federal authorities and had his sentence reduced to 18 months in prison. He entered a minimum security prison on November 10, 1993 to serve his sentence.

This real estate was too valuable to developers to allow it to be forsaken to the poor and the elderly. For years it was like a battle ground with large developers anxious to use the land for grandiose schemes. A Redevelopment Association was formed with the goal of zoning to permit building large condominiums. A moratorium was declared in 1975, and for nine years no new building or repairs were allowed in the South Shore Area. By the time the moratorium was over the land values were very low, most of the elderly had passed away, so developers were able to move in and build the massive condominiums they had aspired to.

South Beach

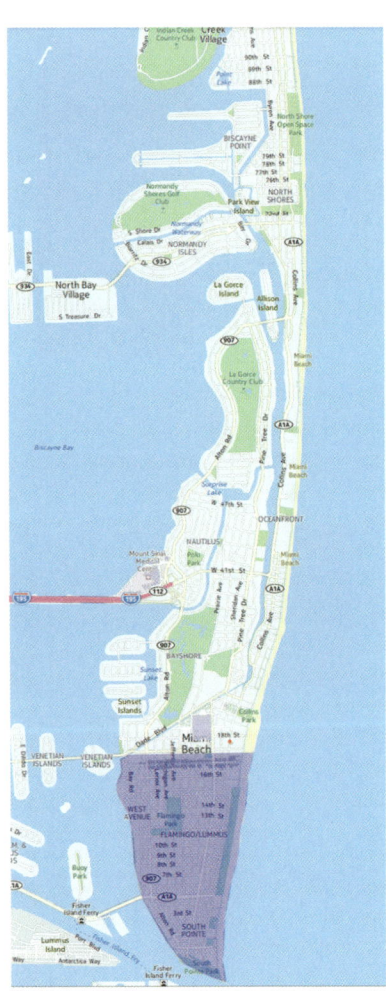

South of Fifth
    Government Cut
    Browns Hotel
    Joe's Stone Crab
    Tap Tap Haitian Restaurant
    Jewish Museum of Florida-FIU

Ocean Drive
    Versace Mansion - Casa Casuarina
    Lummus Park
    Art Deco
    Wolfsonian-FIU
    Mango's Tropical Cafe
    Beach Patrol - Lifeguard Stations

Española Way

Venetian Isles

Lincoln Road
    Miami Beach Convention Center
    Loews / St. Moritz
    New World Symphony
    Holocaust Memorial
    Miami City Ballet

One could easily claim that the most intense history of Miami Beach has occurred in what is today known as South Beach; the twenty-three most southerly blocks of the city. Partially due to its close proximity to the City of Miami across the bay, South Beach has been the object of agricultural, touristic and real estate development plans and schemes since the late 1800's.

Farmed by John Collins, platted by the Lummus brothers, hyped and developed by Carl Fisher; South Beach has seen frenzied land booms, a giant hurricane in 1926, the explosion of an art deco themed era, the advent of a submarine-prowling World War II, a crime wave in the 1980's that had the area labeled as the most crime-ridden city in the U.S. The deterioration nearly doomed South Beach's now famous Art Deco neighborhood.

But a new wave of prosperity was ushered in through the efforts of activist Barbara Capitman and the organization she founded, the Miami Design Preservation League (MDPL).

Today, South Beach is one of the world's most prosperous and popular locations. It is the centerpiece of the Miami area's multi-billion dollar tourism and real estate industry. It is a bustling center of international culture and fashion and it is the embodiment of Miami Beach's undeniable swagger.

South of Fifth

When you walk south on Ocean Drive, you do not need a map or a street sign to inform you that another neighborhood is emerging. Lummus Park, fronting the beach from 15th Street, ends and a large apartment building comes into sight blocking direct access to the ocean. South of Fifth begins a change in the character of Ocean Drive and an entirely different lifestyle and ambiance now is evident.

It is in this area, South of Fifth, where the current history of Miami Beach had its beginning. In 1903, the Army Corps of Engineers, at the urging of Henry Flagler, dredged an opening through the mangroves to create Government Cut, to provide easier access to the Port of Miami.

Many people rowed across Biscayne Bay to visit the beach. Soon ferries began to ply the waters, and in 1904 a bathing casino was built. People could rent a swimming suit for 25 cents.

Brothers J.E. and J.N. Lummus sold small parcels of land to anyone who was white and could afford to pay. This was in contrast to the other large developers of Miami Beach, John Collins and Carl Fisher, who restricted sales of their land to Gentiles only.

On March 26, 1915, Fisher, Collins and the Lummus Brothers met at the Ocean Realty Company in order to incorporate Miami Beach as a town. It was incorporated as the City of Miami Beach on May 21, 1917 by an act of the Florida legislature.

In 1915, Browns Hotel was opened and in 1918, Joe's Restaurant, later to be named Joe's Stone Crab, opened its doors. Small hotels and apartment buildings soon populated the area.

In the 1930's, a frenzy of building occurred in response to the popularity of Miami Beach as an hospitable place for winter-weary northerners, now beset by economic woes caused by the Great Depression. While unemployment in the nation reached unprecedented levels those who were employed were in search of warm weather and inexpensive hotels.

After World War II, Miami Beach became a popular destination. As Ocean Drive north of Fifth grew with hotels and apartments for tourists, the area south of Fifth became home to many Jewish people who were welcomed and allowed to follow their religion and create a comfortable lifestyle. Synagogues were built, delis were opened, schools and libraries and parks became part of the landscape. South of Fifth became a refuge for thousands of people seeking a new life for themselves. Many of these people lived on retirement pay and social security. It was one of the lowest income areas in the country.

This frugal, comfortable lifestyle could not exist for long. This desired property, in one of the most favored spots on Earth, became a battleground between land developers and the residents of the area.

This was land that was worth millions of dollars and cried out for development.

In the 1970's, while the preservationists were battling to save the Art Deco District north of Fifth, a redevelopment movement began south of Fifth. Even though many of the buildings were in good condition, the area was declared "blighted" by the City Commission in 1975. The arguments reached such a fevered pitch that a moratorium on new building or renovation was called by the city commissioners. This moratorium lasted for nine years and the area fell into great disrepair. Landlords would not make any repairs because the property values were falling so rapidly.

In addition, the revolution in Cuba affected South Florida as tens of thousands of refugees came to the United States. These refugees were referred to as Marielitos. Included were about 15,000 former prisoners and residents of mental institutions released by the Castro government. The U.S. federal government paid the rent for these refugees and many of them came to the low rent district of South Shore. The crime rate soared and the elderly were easy prey for the criminals and drug addicts who also inhabited this area.

In order to address the problem of the decaying neighborhood of the area south of Fifth, the City Commission sent out an RFP (Request for Proposal) to rejuvenate the area. A group of citizens responded by forming the (RDA) Redevelopment Association. This group created a master plan which included grand hotels, elaborate restaurants and shops, luxurious homes, huge condominiums and canals which would have gondolas cruising the waterways. While these plans were being articulated, the people living in the neighborhood were in panic. Where would they go? What would become of them?

The grandiose redevelopment plan was never approved, but the land became so inexpensive, as the decline escalated, that large developers bought it at bargain prices and soon condominiums were built which dominated the landscape. What does remain of this grandiose scheme is the Miami Beach Marina. Building of this Marina was begun in 1977, when the city broke ground for a breakwater and two piers. This was meant to be the hub of the new development.

The elderly people were displaced or died of old age. The old boardinghouses and apartment buildings soon disappeared. The rocking chairs of the elderly were gone and running and bike paths were created.

At the very tip of South Pointe is a public park that consists of 17.5 acres that was dedicated on March 22, 2009. It was developed at a cost of $22.4 million dollars. The land was donated by the Federal government to Miami Beach. It originally housed police horse stables, and a building for harbor pilots.

Government Cut

The early settlers of the new town of Miami were aware of the legendary white sand beaches that stretched down the length of what we know today as South Beach. For those who had a full day's time and a reliable boat, a trip to Miami Beach was a possibility. They would depart from the Miami River, drop all the way down around the Cape Florida lighthouse on Key Biscayne and make their way up the coast to Miami Beach. It was an all day venture in pursuit of fun at the seashore.

For seagoing commerce, Miami was not an attractive port of call because of the long arduous trip involved. Henry Flagler wanted to create a passageway from Biscayne Bay to the ocean. In 1901, he sent emissaries to Washington D.C. to lobby for assistance in creating a channel running from west to east across the peninsula. Congress provided $300,000 to cut an 18-foot deep channel and Flagler provided a like amount to deepen the channel from his wharf in Miami to Miami Beach. The cut was completed on March 14th, 1905, connecting the bay and ocean.

The residents of Miami turned out en masse, about 3500 people, to celebrate the great day. John Sewell, the Mayor of Miami, declared the event to be a holiday. Excitement reached a fevered pitch as the dredge moved to close the gap between the bay and the ocean; suddenly dredging ceased, the big dipper would not move an inch; disappointment swept through the crowd. Perplexed but undaunted, Mayor Sewell picked up a spade and with great energy attacked the remaining sand-bar that prevented the union of the bay and the ocean. In about half-an-hour a stream of water from the bay joined the Atlantic Ocean. Within a few hours the flow widened to nearly ten feet. The crowd was thrilled. The next day the cut had reached a width of 500 feet.

The access to Miami through Government Cut created a great increase in shipping, for commerce and tourism. New islands were formed from the dredging spoils; Dodge, Lummus, Sam's Island and a few other smaller islands. With the growth of South Florida, additional land was needed to expand port activities. In 1960, the City of Miami passed a resolution to create the new Port of Miami. The location of the Port was on Dodge Island which was expanded and joined to other islands. Miami is now considered the "Cruise Capital of the World" and the "Cargo Gateway of the Americas."

Government Cut is the ocean harbor entrance and exit for all the cruise ships from Miami. When the cut was completed, it created a small island, separated from Miami Beach. That Island is now known as Fisher Island and can only be reached from the causeway by a private ferry.

Browns Hotel

South Beach's very first hotel certainly couldn't be compared to the architecturally distinct masterpieces that would rise on Miami Beach in the decades to come. It was a simple wooden building that filled the entire, long, narrow residential lot purchased by the hotel's founder, William J. Brown, in 1914. With its sturdy Dade County Pine framing and practical design, Browns' Hotel, originally called the Atlantic Beach Hotel, looks something more like a stage piece for an old Western movie set than a resort hotel in America's new tropical playground.

William Brown, a Scottish immigrant and plumber by trade, saw an opportunity where others had made promises. Although he was financially only able to build on the most modest of scales, Brown beat the great developers to the starting line for Miami Beach's first hotel.

Interestingly, either Brown was a brilliant pitchman or a skillful fabricator. He claimed that when he began to construct the foundation for his hotel he came upon the skeleton of an old, 125-foot ship buried beneath the sand. Speculation was that it was an old Spanish Galleon or pirate ship that some long-ago hurricane had driven up onto the beach. Since he couldn't afford to excavate the ship, he claimed to have built the hotel right over the wreck. Since the hotel's foundation was built over the top of the still intact ship below, no one would be able to dispute Brown's claim. It made for a great story to tell guests of the hotel. As fate would have it, Brown made an oversight that no one could have anticipated. Eventually, his hotel would be picked up and moved so that his engaging claim could be either refuted or substantiated.

Originally, Brown constructed his hotel something akin to a stilt structure. The first floor was only seven feet in height, just tall enough for a person to change into and out of a swimming suit in the ground floor changing room. Although the first floor was only used for changing, Brown still covered the sides, giving the appearance of a full ground floor to the building. The concrete piers of the first floor were almost in collapse by the modern era but the wooden second floor looked like it had just been built.

William Brown sold his hotel in 1935, twenty years after its 1915 debut. Brown later became a prominent local banker. Shortly after the hotel's sale, the Browns disappeared. It is assumed that it was demolished in the quick pace of Miami Beach development.

It would not be until 1992 that the Browns would "reappear". Short of an elaborate, decades-long magic illusion, how could this happen? The story follows that as Ocean Drive went from a sandy foot path to a full-fledged street, the setback called for the Browns protruding, enclosed front porch entry to be demolished to allow for enough room for street expansion. Once sheared of its front porch, the Browns Hotel was quickly modernized into an art deco styled building. Coats of plaster were adhered to the façade and all the outside surfaces of the building. Everyone generally assumed that in the fast-paced building spree that characterized Miami Beach in the 1930s, this new building was a quick addition to the growing collection of art deco structures in the area.

This would be the assumption until the ferocious Hurricane Andrew passed by South Beach on its path of destruction over Key Biscayne in August of 1992. A chunk of plaster was dislodged from the side of the building. Curiously, the gap revealed the well-preserved remains of a much older wooden structure beneath the plaster. What was this place? It was Browns Hotel. Miami Beach's first hotel was never torn down. It had been the subject of a quick and thoroughly convincing modernization.

With the rediscovery of the Browns Hotel, talk soon turned to whether to save it or even if it could be saved. The Miami Beach Planning Department under William Cary made it known that the city would fight to save the building. Others made the case that it was too expensive and too far gone to restore.

Ultimately, it was the bold risk-taking instincts of owners Nelson Fox and Bob Mooney and the talent of Restoration Architect Allan Shulman that would win the day. In a three year restoration, Shulman had the entire building lifted and moved back 13 feet. Thus he was able to rebuild the original front porch, sheared off all those years ago during the expansion of Ocean Drive. Also, he was able to, once and for all, investigate William Browns original claim of the beached ship. Hiring archaeologists to dig a transept under the hotel to see if the ship story bore any physical evidence, the search yielded nothing.

Impressed by the intricate wooden construction of the building, Shulman hired a firm specializing in the restoration of wooden buildings, to bring Browns Hotel back to life.

After the first floor was lifted from its original 7 foot height to its present 10 foot height to add sufficient spaciousness, the space was leased to Prime 112, a restaurant that became one of the hottest on South Beach and one of the most profitable in the country.

Joe's Stone Crab

Joe Weiss moved from New York City to Miami Beach in 1913. Miami Beach was incorporated as a town in 1915. For a hundred years Joe's Stone Crab Restaurant and the City of Miami Beach grew up together enjoying good times and suffering through bad ones. Joe had asthma while living in New York. His doctor suggested a move to a warmer climate. At the time Joe was a waiter and his wife, Jennie was a cook. They had a son Jesse who was born in 1907.

In 1913, after borrowing fifty dollars from his life-insurance policy, Joe headed for Florida. He first went to Miami, but not feeling any better, he left the next day. He took a ferry from Miami to Miami Beach, where the clear air seemed to suit him. At the time there were about 30 to 40 people living in Miami Beach. A swimming pavilion, known as Smith's Bathing Casino, was located on the beach where people from Miami could come to enjoy the ocean and the pool. The casino was the place to rent a locker to change into swimming clothes. Before long, Joe began to operate a lunch stand from the casino. He soon sent for Jennie and six-year old Jesse, Joe and Jennie operated the restaurant at Smith's for about five years. In 1918, they bought a small house on Biscayne Street and set up their own restaurant simply called, Joe's Restaurant.

The early 1900's was a boom time in Miami Beach and Joe's restaurant flourished. For eight years it was the only restaurant on Miami Beach. In 1913 the Collins Bridge was built which connected the beach to the mainland. At the time this was the longest wooden bridge in the world. By 1920, the permanent year-round population was 644. A causeway was built in 1920, which opened the flood-gates to Miami Beach which soon became known as "America's Winter Playground".

The restaurant was open for breakfast, lunch and dinner. Mosquitoes were a great nuisance, and employees of Joe's tried to keep them away with smudge pots. The heat in the summer months was almost unbearable, so ceiling fans were installed. The season was short, about twelve weeks long.

Two events really catapulted Miami Beach into becoming a major destination. One was the opening of the Hialeah Race Track, west of Miami, the other was the start of the motion picture industry. Palm Beach was the winter residence of many of the tycoons at the time and they would take the train to Miami for the races. The crews of the movie industry, which started about 1921, would eat all their meals at Joe's Restaurant. No doubt about it, Joe was in the right place at the right time.

Stone crabs were abundant in Biscayne Bay, but were considered inedible. In 1921 James Allison built an aquarium on the bay side and Fifth Street. He invited an ichthyologist, a researcher from Harvard, to visit the aquarium. One day this man brought a burlap bag full of stone crabs into Joe's Restaurant and asked Joe if he ever served them to his diners. Joe said that no one would eat them. However, he did experiment with cooking them, He eventually threw them into a pot of boiling water and tried eating them hot. No good. They were mushy. Next he tried them cold, and the nice firm meat was appealing. Joe created a mustard sauce and that was just right.

Stone crabs became a great success. It wasn't too long before the dredging of the Bay, to allow entry to big ships, resulted in the loss of habitat for stone crabs in that area. Now, most Florida stone crabs come from the Keys or the Gulf Coast. Joe's has a processing plant near Naples and supplies crabs to other restaurants. Strict laws regulate the way stone crabs are harvested. Since claws regenerate themselves, only one claw is removed and the crab must be returned to the water.

The personalities of Joe, Jennie and later, Jesse, permeated the atmosphere at the restaurant. Jennie was known as a tough person, who either liked you or didn't. She was known to refuse service to people if she objected to their values. On the other hand, some of her favorites were of dubious character. She favored Al Capone, (who went by the name of Al Brown) the gangster; since he was always polite. He sent flowers to her on Mother's Day. If a man came in with a woman, not his wife, Jennie would not let them stay.

Joe died in 1980 and Jesse and Jennie operated the restaurant together. Jennie died in 1988, and then Jesse was the one to run things. Jesse spent four years in the army. He was a colorful man, who loved horse racing and women. He had seven marriages, finally settling down with wife number seven, Grace, for more than fifty years.

When Jesse took over the restaurant in 1945, it was close to bankruptcy. Grace worked with Jesse to pay every bill which included a $3,500 bill for meat. There were also some old gambling debts that Joe had incurred. It took four years and every bill was paid. During this time, the name was changed from Joe's Restaurant to Joe's Stone Crab.

After one hundred years, Joe's Stone Crab remains family owned. The current President of the company, Stephen Sawitz, is proud of his heritage and the significant role that the restaurant has played in the history of Miami Beach. He is the Great Great Grandson of Joe Weiss and is the fourth generation of the family to operate the company.

Tap Tap Haitian Restaurant

Katherine Kean, a New York born artist, film maker and philanthropist, who had travelled widely in Haiti, gained an appreciation for the culture, spirit and artistry of the Haitian people. She had a great desire to acknowledge her respect for these attributes. Kean's ideas would galvanize around an unoccupied two-story flop-house on Fifth Street in South Beach. The building would be renovated using the skills and talents of Haitian refugees. A restaurant would be created serving Haitian cuisine, fussed over by Haitian chefs and wait staff and decorated by Haitian artists.

The opportunity for democratic elections brought Jean Bertrand Aristide, a former Haitian priest, who had worked among the poor, into the presidency. Katherine opened her new establishment in 1994. By then, President Aristide had been deposed in a coup d'etat. Now, the building that was supposed to showcase Haitian culture had a more compelling purpose. It was to become a refuge for exiles from Haiti to America as well as a showcase for Haitian culture.

It was Kean's idea to correct the view of Haiti as a basket-case country, poor and uncivilized sending thousands of fearful people out on the seas in rickety boats. Instead, she wanted to show the history of a people who had aided the American Revolution with arms and men and, following the revolution, had become the second independent republic in the Western Hemisphere She wanted people to know that the Haitian people instituted the first and only successful slave revolution in the New World. Also, the Haitian revolution had ended Napoleon's ambitions for the New World and prompted the sale of French Louisiana to the U.S., doubling the size of the country.

In 1994, with the return of dictatorship to Haiti, many prominent intellectuals, political leaders and artists went into exile and came to Miami. The new home away from home for some of these exiles would be the two-story historic apartment house created by Kean. It can be recognized by its light purple exterior and its quaint, inviting walk-up porch. In front of the porch, Kean placed a vehicle which is a replica of the charming colorful taxis once prevalent on the streets of Port au Prince.   The local slang for these taxis: Taps Taps.

The first floor was designed with a bar, various attractive seating rooms, a kitchen and an area for live entertainment. The second floor would be used for art shows, book signings and political meetings. It is on the walls, floors, ceilings and every available surface of the building that things really get interesting. Kean recruited five Haitian artists living and working in Miami to create the desired effect. The walls, ceilings, floors, tables and chairs are adorned with folk art depicting scenes from the Haitian countryside and representations of the various gods who permeate Haitian popular culture.

This is reflected in a popular saying that Haiti is 90% Catholic and 100% Vodou. If you notice the reference to the Kreyol (Creole) spelling "Vodou", which differs from the French spelling "Vodoun" and differs yet again from the common English reference "Voodoo" we are informed that the "Hollywood version" (Voodoo) is offensive and would never be spelled this way in any serious Haitian writing. The Vodou gods represented throughout the restaurant include Damballa, the snake god: Papa Gede, guardian of the dead and masters of libido and Papa Legba who governs the threshold to the spirit world. Kean tells us that no one fears the images and that they represent only positive elements of Haitian spiritualism.

When it came time to choose the menu for Tap Tap, there was lively discussion which centered on class distinctions. In Haiti, restaurants would serve French food. Simple staples of Haitian daily food were found only in the home. Tap Tap sides with home food. The chef would start you off with an appetizer such as Soup Joumous (pumpkin soup) or Akra (malang fritters). A healthy portion of a Haitian staple such as rice, beans, bananas, eggplant, cabbage, carrots, chicken, fish, goat or guinea hen would follow. These would often be spiced with Scotch bonnet pepper cloves, coconut, sour orange, lime, salt and pepper or thyme. A beverage choice would include tropical fruit juices like Ji Grenadya (passion fruit juice), Ji Korosol (soursop), or a tropical fruit punch. For dessert there is Benyen (banana fritters), Blan Mange (coconut) or Pen Patat (sweet potato pie).

On a Saturday night many Haitian exiles gather for a night of music and discussion. Katherine has provided a safe haven for these displaced people.

The Jewish Museum of Florida

The origins of the Jewish Museum of Florida can be traced back to the efforts of Marcia Jo Zerivitz who spent twenty years, beginning in 1985, criss-crossing and zig-zagging across the state seeking the roots of Jewish people as they migrated from other states and other nations. It was generally assumed that the population of Jewish people was largely a movement in the 1950's, but Marcia's investigations indicate that Jews were among the early settlers, some coming as early as the 1500's. It is because of her relentless pursuit of Jewish history that the Jewish Museum exists today, housed in two historic buildings on Washington Avenue in South Beach.

The museum chronicles Jewish history, since 1763, much of which was uncovered by Marcia as she traveled from one corner of the state to the other, logging about 100,000 miles interviewing and collecting artifacts. Not a historian by formal education, Marcia collaborated with many historians in the state. In practice she became a master historian, meticulously following every lead until she had enough information and material to mount an exhibit which traveled to 13 cities from 1990 until 1994. This had become a grassroots movement.

The traveling exhibit became the foundation of the MOSAIC Project which is housed in the Museum and includes photographs, artifacts and oral histories. Two side by side buildings constitute the Museum. The first building opened in 1995 in what was a former synagogue built in 1936. The building had served its congregation for fifty years, then was left abandoned. When Marcia first saw the building in 1992, it was in a total state of disrepair. The roof had fallen in, the windows were broken, dead animals were rotting, the floor was destroyed by termites. Yet, Marcia loved the structure of the building and determined to find a way to restore it to its former glory. She mounted a fund raising campaign in a race against the bulldozer. As it turns out her efforts ended up saving the very first project of celebrated Miami Beach architect Henry Hohauser. A two year restoration took place costing $1.5 million dollars.   In 2007 the second building was occupied in what was an original synagogue built in l929. The location of the original synagogues were chosen because at that time Jews were not allowed to live north of Fifth Street.   Before the construction of these synagogues, Jews were denied permission to construct a building. They had to take the ferry across Biscayne Bay to attend religious services in Miami. The museum tells the stories of people, their struggles, their dreams and their accomplishments. "It's purpose is to provide a sense of identity and to serve as a reminder of who we were and who we are and who we aspire to become", according to Marcia. She believes that we are our memories and history is our collective memory.

Marcia resigned as director in 2011 and was succeeded by Jo Ann Arnowitz.

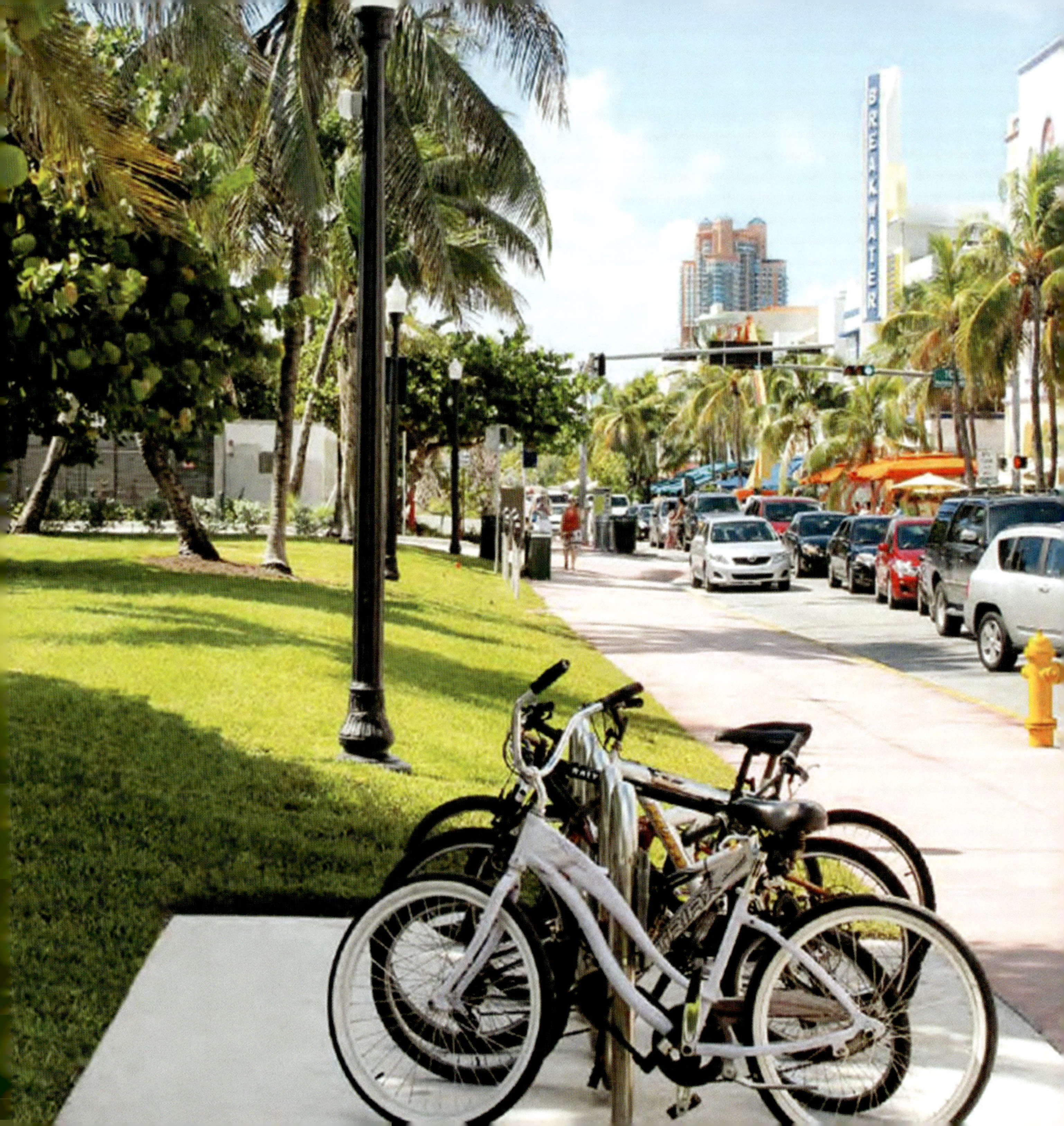
BREAKWATER

Ocean Drive

    The Lummus brothers, J.E. and J.N., bankers in Miami, recognized the potential of beach development if a bridge were built to connect the mainland with the beach. When John Collins asked for a loan to build such a bridge so that he could transport agricultural products to Miami for shipment to northern markets, they were happy to oblige.

    They purchased 600 acres of Miami Beach land, in 1912, from what is now Lincoln Road to the tip of South Beach. It was land inhabited by millions of creatures; large and small, from alligators to swarms of mosquitoes. The first task was to tame the jungle to make it habitable for humans. It was the beach that held the great allure, and it was on this property where Ocean Drive has its beginning, from First Street to Fifteenth Street.

    The Lummuses created an atmosphere where middle income people could enjoy the beach. They sold smaller parcels of land to accommodate modest apartment buildings, moderate hotels and restaurants. They bought ferry boats to bring visitors across the bay from Miami for a day's outing. They had salesmen on the ferries to promote the sale of property. Most importantly, they created a public park stretching oceanside across their property from 5th to 15th Streets.

    Unlike Carl Fisher who wanted to create a lavish environment for the super-rich, or John Collins and his son-in-law who were appealing to the generally wealthy upper-income people, the Lummuses wanted to create a haven, affordable for working people, so they sub-divided their property into small parcels at low prices.

    In 1915, when Miami Beach was incorporated as a city, the Lummuses sold their beachfront property to the city for a park for little more than they had paid for it; $40,000. The stipulation for the sale to the City was that it never be allowed to build homes, hotels or other commercial buildings on the park land. Across from Lummus Park became the neighborhood for small hotels and outdoor restaurants. This established the character of the area, later to become world famous as the Art Deco district of South Beach.

    The land north of 15th became home to large hotels and condominiums, allowing for little direct access to the beach. The policies of selling smaller parcels of land at more moderate prices and providing for an enduring park, created the foundation for Ocean Drive as it now exists; home to a lively neighborhood of smaller hotels, restaurants and apartment buildings, friendly to pedestrians, bike riders and beach goers.

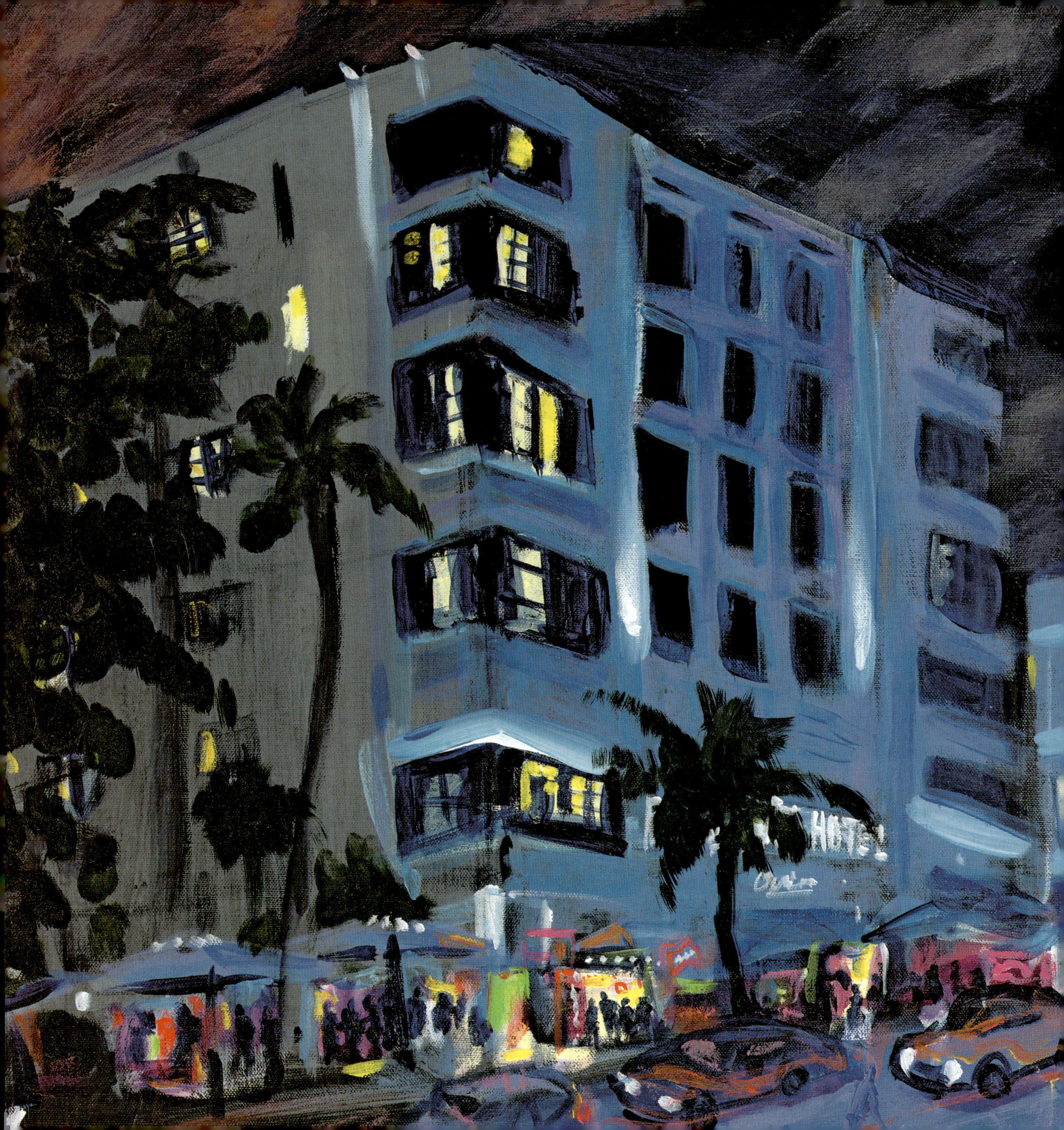

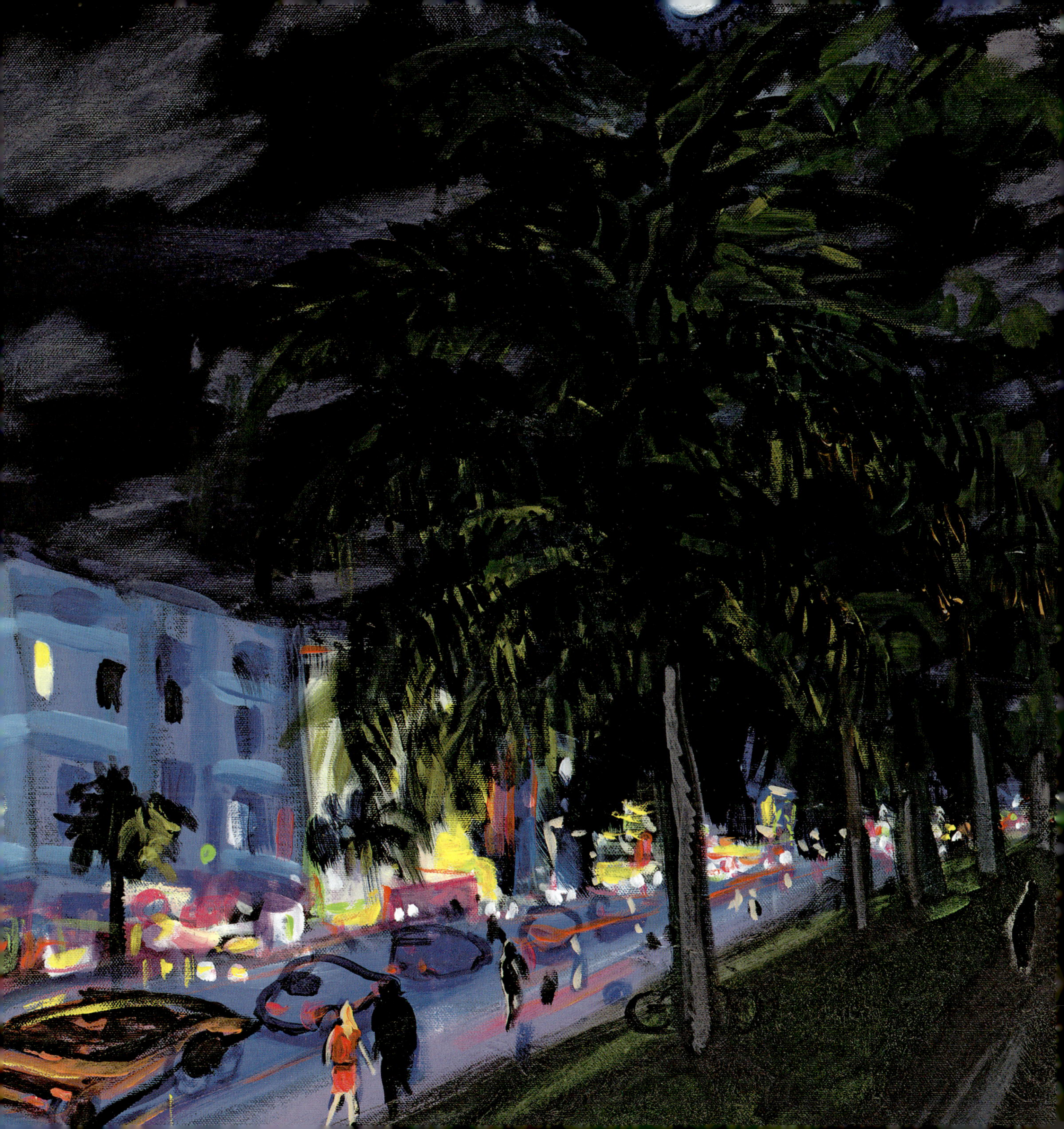

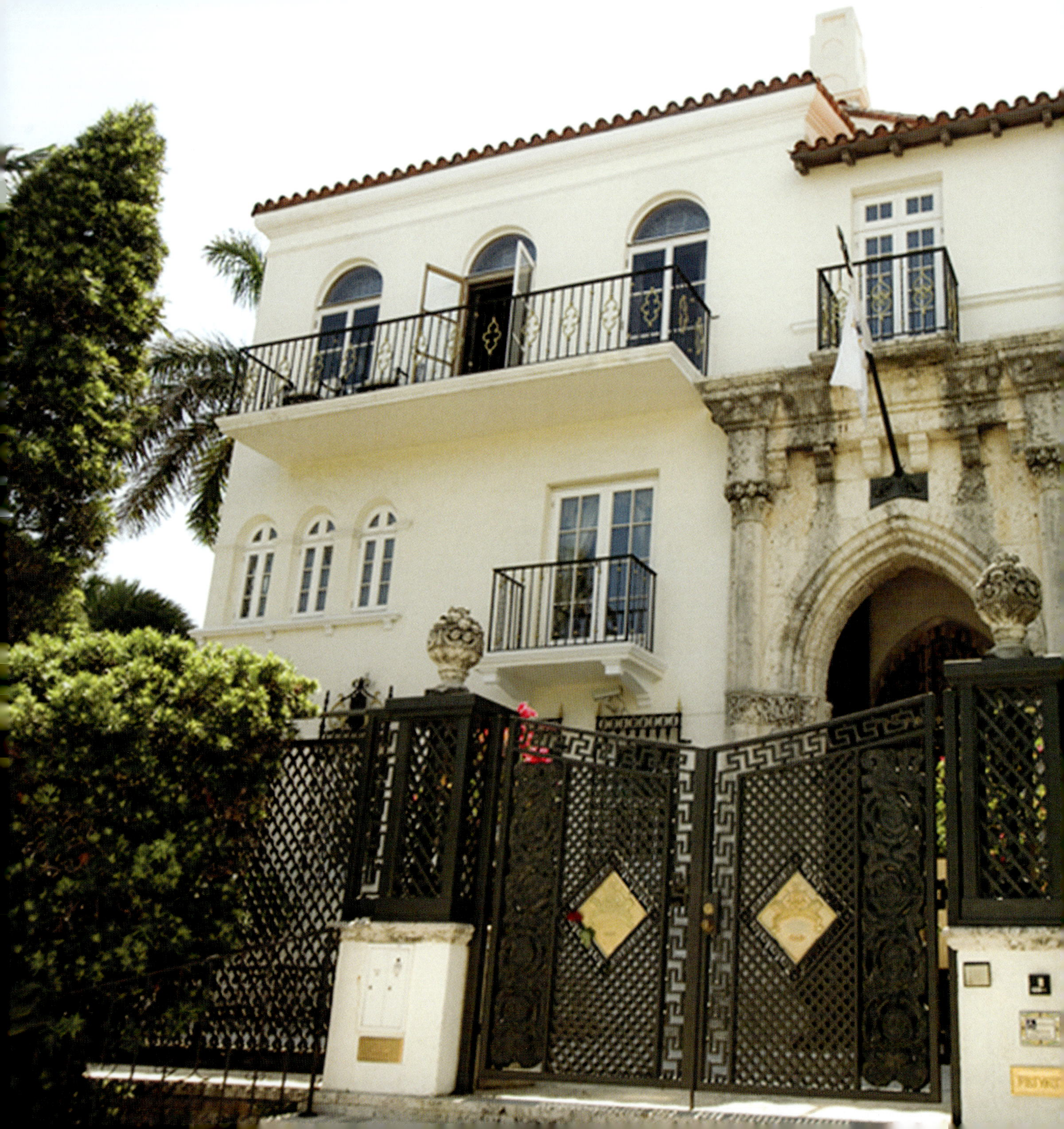

Casa Casuarina

On 1116 Ocean Drive, in Miami Beach there is one of the most legendary residences in the world. It was originally named Casa Casuarina. Built in 1930 by Charles Boulton and Alden Freeman, two bachelors; one (Freeman) an eccentric millionaire and the other (Boulton) a younger landscape designer. The residence has always been equated with extravagance. It was named after a lone Australian Pine (Casuarina tree) left standing after the Great Hurricane of 1926. The name was also inspired by a collection of six short stories from author W. Somerset Maugham's "The Casuarina Tree" about a group of British adventurers in Malaya. Freeman was a great admirer of Maugham's writings.

Casa Casuarina was a masterpiece. The house was designed as an exact replica of the Alcazar de Colon in Santo Domingo (Dominican Republic). That residence, constructed between 1506 and 1510, was the home of Diego Columbus (son of Christopher Columbus) and Doña Maria de Toledo, niece of King Ferdinand and Queen Isabella of Spain. A brick from this original residence is prominently featured in the front façade of today's Villa. Boulton and Freeman incorporated great works of art and sculpture throughout the building. One exceptional work, the "Kneeling Aphrodite" by California sculptor Vuk Vuchinich, still graces the residence. Other original statuary, found in the palatial home's Spanish-style, three-story inner courtyard, includes busts of great leaders from every continent throughout the ages; philosophers, political leaders and explorers.

By 1935, the name was changed from Casa Casuarina to Amsterdam Palace after its new owner, Jac Amsterdam. The name Amsterdam Palace lingered on for decades. In the early 1980s, British tour operator Bryn Roden moved into the Penthouse of a now very subdued mansion. The house had long since declined to become a bohemian low-rent apartment building. Every Friday night featured a pot (as in marijuana) party and the palatial property was subdivided into one-bedroom and studio apartments with a mix of young and old tenants. Roden and his partner had to deal with leaks, frequently blown transformers and a stream of requests from the button next to the steel gate covering the front archway to be allowed entry. From the Penthouse, Roden could throw a switch to open the gate.

The building was controlled by Gerry Sanchez, a cigar-smoking wheeler dealer in the early days of South Beach, who drove around in a white Rolls Royce. Sanchez would often ask Roden for rent in advance. Roden would pay him three months in advance for two

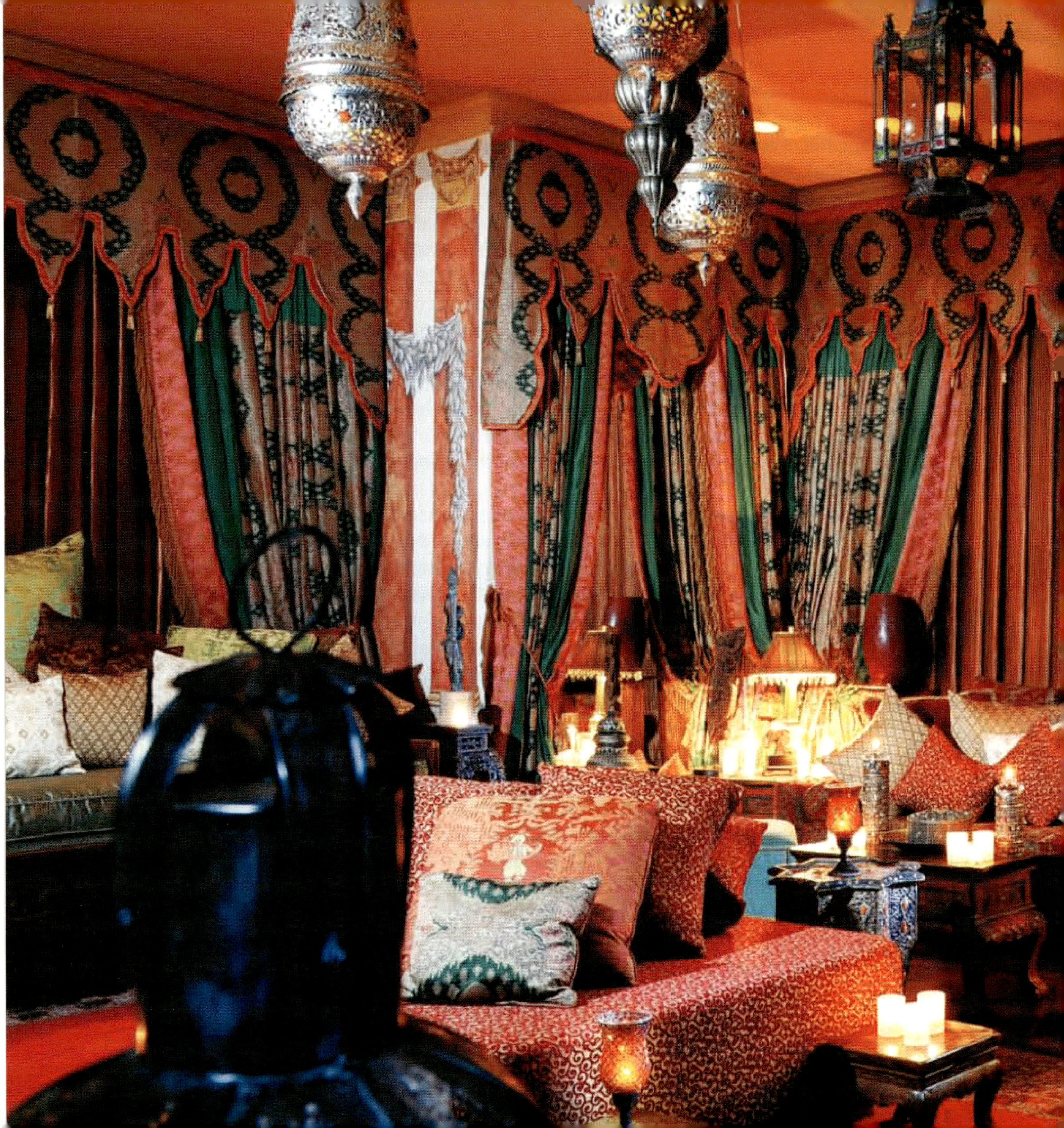

The Moroccan Room at The Villa.

LUMMUS PARK
CITY OF
MIAMI BEACH

Lummus Park

From 5th Street to 15th Street on the eastern (beach) side of Ocean Drive, there is a linear park called Lummus Park. Designed in 1912 by visionaries who understood the value of public places, Lummus Park remains at the epicenter of South Beach outdoor life.

The Lummus Brothers, J.E. and J.N. Lummus, were very successful early developers of Miami Beach. Their plan called for the creation of a "seaside community of the proletariat." The word "proletariat" might strike us as odd in today's parlance but, coined before the Bolshevik Revolution, the word was a lot less weighted in 1912. Nevertheless, a modern attempt to excise the word was narrowly defeated at City Hall. The Lummus Brothers were merely indicating that their lots would be affordable to the average buyer. For this reason, the lots were platted only 50 feet wide by 150 feet deep.

The subdivision created by the Lummus Brothers ran from Ocean Drive to Washington Avenue (east to west) and from 6th Street to Government Cut (north to south). Buyers who committed to purchase in the first year were offered free lots as long as they agreed to erect a building that would meet the developer's standards. This offer created enough momentum to get the development in high gear. From the success of their development, John Lummus (J.N.) went on to become the first mayor of Miami Beach.

Lummus Park, set aside in 1912, was sold to the City of Miami Beach in 1917 for $40,000 dollars, with the stipulation that there be no hotels or any construction in the park. The coral rock wall that currently runs the length of the park was once closer to Ocean Drive. The wall was moved westward over the years. At one time, the wall marked the boundary to the sand. This meant the 1939 Beach Patrol Headquarters was built on the beach, in the sand. Thus, the building did not violate the Lummus Brothers' stipulation about buildings in the park. Knowing that the Beach Patrol Headquarters once sat on the actual beach helps illustrate how much the beach has been added to in subsequent years. It is clear that the hotels of Ocean Drive were once much closer to the ocean, with commanding views that came with such close proximity.

The park was laid out with a central plaza at 10th and Ocean. Curving sidewalks radiated out from the central plaza going north and south. When restrooms were built in the 1930s, they were considered to be in keeping with the spirit of the "no building" requirement.

However, 1954 brought a break with the established covenant that the brothers had left. In 1954, with the opening of the Fontainebleau Hotel in the 40th block of Miami Beach, the small hotels of South Beach were put at a strong disadvantage. These small hotels didn't have the meeting spaces that the Fontainebleau provided. In response to pressure from the small hotels, the City of Miami Beach constructed an auditorium-style building right on top of Lummus Park's central plaza at 10th and Ocean. The building was meant to be a convention center for the small hotels. Over the years, it has been known as the Oceanfront Auditorium, the South Shore Community Center and most recently after a renovation and considerable reduction in size; the Art Deco Welcome Center.

The one consistent feature of the park has been its plantings. The park is famous for its towering palm trees. The original trees were known as Panamanian Talls. After a tree blight in the 1970s, known as lethal yellowing, killed most of South Florida's Panamanian Talls, horticulturalists took the short, but blight-resistant Malaysian Coconut tree and cross-bred it with the Panamanian Tall. The resulting blight-resistant coconut tree is known as the Maypan (for Malaysian/Panamanian) and continues to dominate the park today. The other species to be found in good number in the park is the native Sea Grape tree, so-called for the large groupings of "grapes" that it produces.

Lummus Park continues to serve the function that it has always served. The park, set aside for public use sees joggers, skaters, tourists, volleyball players, swimmers, vendors, sun-worshipers, homeless, lovers, artists and the full spectrum of South Beach life. It has fulfilled its mission as a core part of the Lummus Brothers' well-conceived "seaside community."

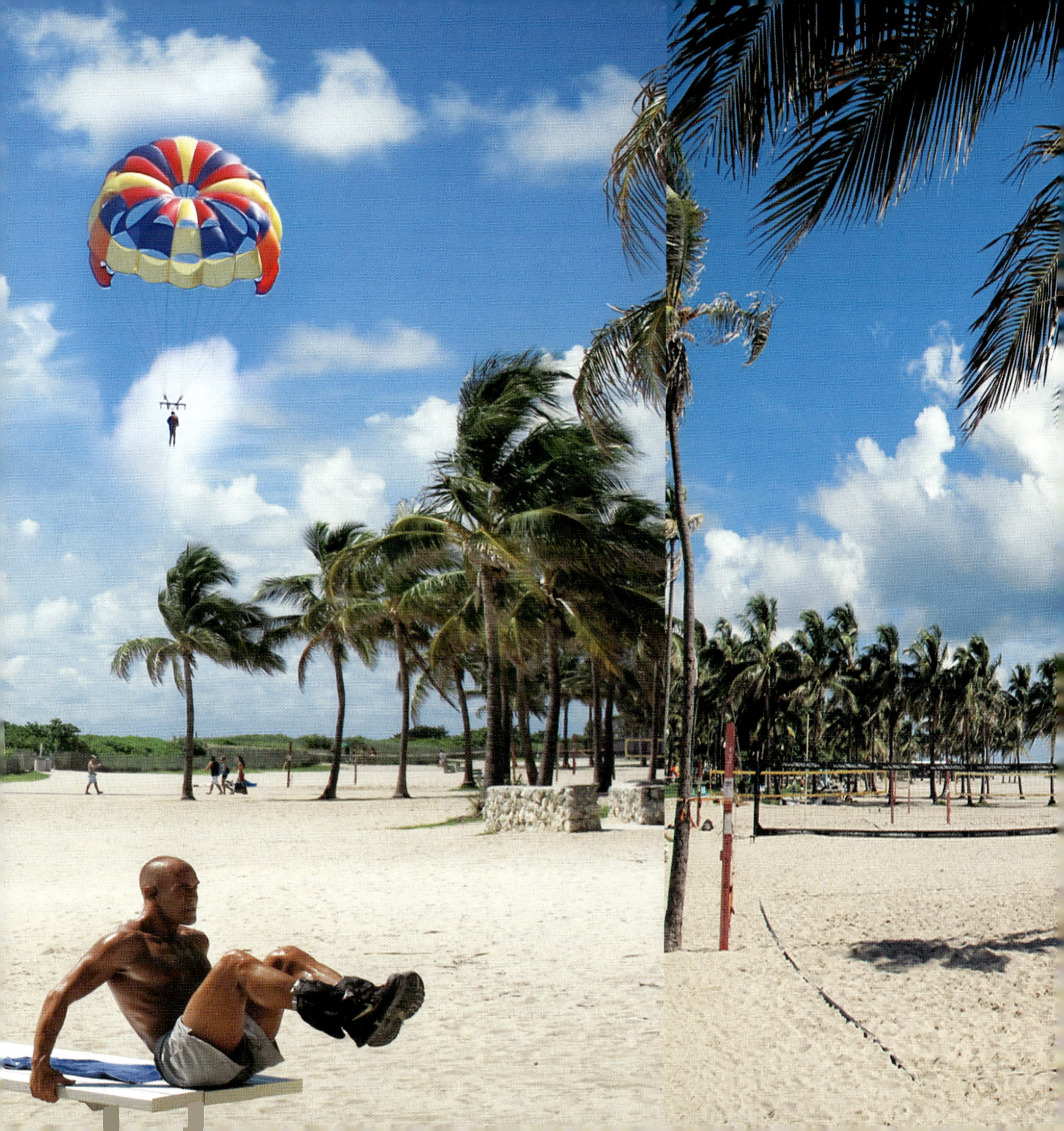

PARK CENTRAL HOTEL

Art Deco

The Great Depression starting in 1929 had a surprising effect on Miami Beach. While it devastated the fortunes of millions of people throughout the nation, including that of Carl Fisher, and called a halt to the wild frenzy of development that began in the early twenties, with a brief respite due to the massive hurricane of 1926, it heralded another boom in South Beach.

The tropical climate still had wide appeal, some people had some money, and more than ever they desired relief from the northern states, not just from the cold, but also from the gloomy economic woes. Developers responded by creating a building boom of smaller, less expensively built hotels and apartments to cater to smaller tourist budgets. Architects were schooled in a new type of design, abandoning the Mediterranean for a more pragmatic modern style, responding to the new technological age. The façades of the buildings were ornate and reflected a nautical theme, using port-holes, jaunty curves and stream-lined entry ways.

Great architecture was born, and competition was created with several architects, leading the way. Among them were Henry Hohauser and L.Murray Dixon, who each created hundreds of hotels, along Ocean Drive and neighboring streets. While they were competitive and created a new building frenzy, it was generally a friendly competition because there was plenty of work for everyone. They performed much the same as the participants in an orchestra, each striving for excellence yet creating a whole larger than the sum of its parts. In 1938, it was reported that 77 hotels had been built in the prior two years. Collectively the structures built in this area became known as Art Deco. This great period of activity came to an end when WWII erupted and the hotels were taken over for military use.

One of the great hotels built in 1939, designed by Hohauser was the Cardozo, named after a Jewish Supreme Court Justice, Benjamin Cardozo of the Franklin Delano Roosevelt administration. The Cardozo thrived for several decades, but followed in the pattern of the rest of the neighborhood when the decline pervaded.

When Barbara Capitman and her sons, went on the crusade to save the Art Deco area they bought the Cardozo and it became the center of activity for the MDPL (The Miami Design Preservation League) activities. Andrew Capitman signed a contract for $800,000 for the hotel. Eventually, Capitman owned seven hotels, but it was a real estate venture that he could not maintain. All the hotels were sold in 1983.

Emilio and Gloria Esteban purchased the Cardozo, for $5,000,000, in 1992.

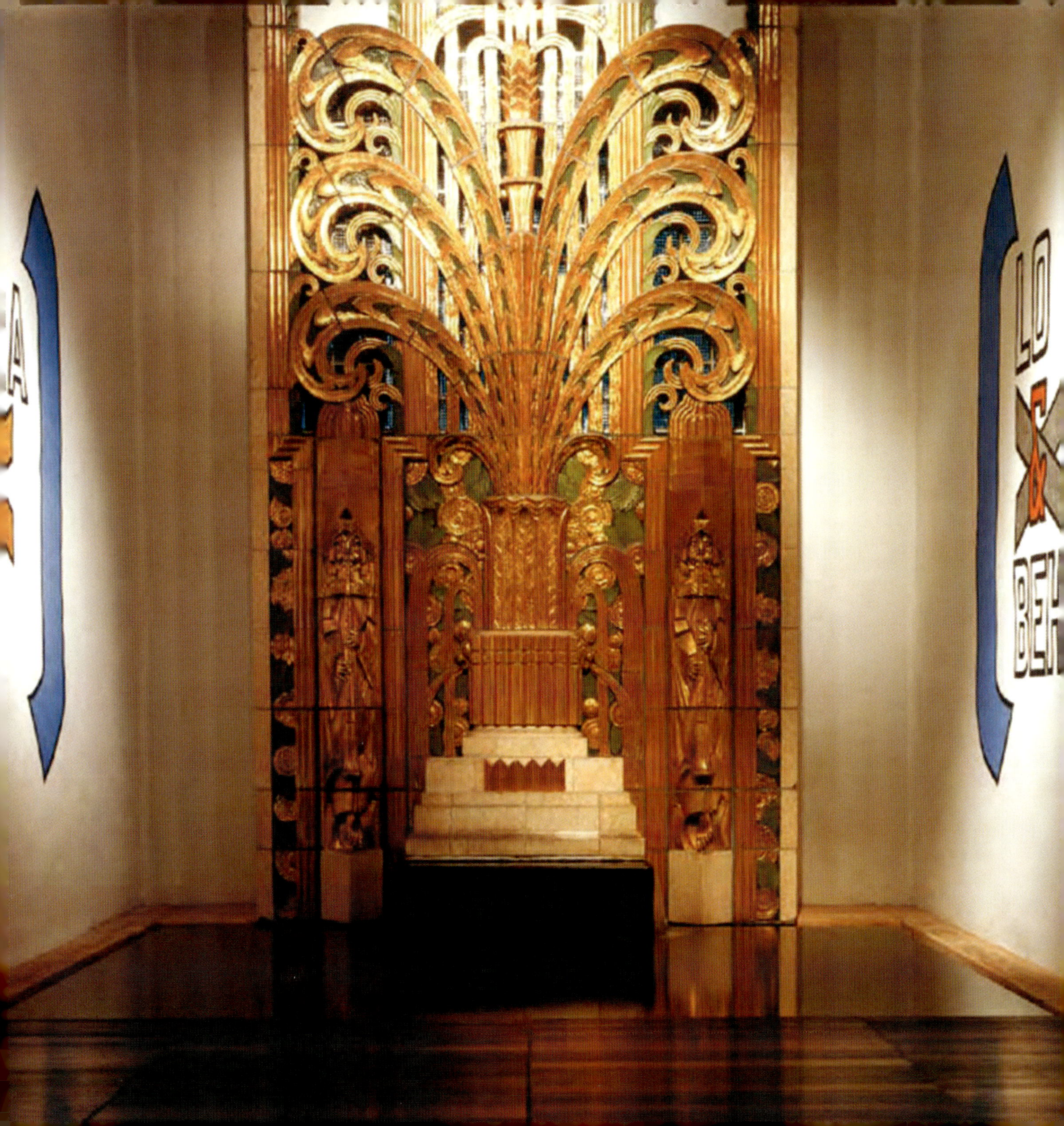

Wolfsonian-FIU

The story of the Wolfsonian-FIU is ultimately the story of a collector. No ordinary collector, but the scion of a wealthy family with vast holdings in movie theaters and television stations. Mitchell, "Micky" Wolfson Jr., grew up in the glamorous and visually stimulating world surrounding his family's business. He attended Princeton as an undergraduate and received a graduate degree from Johns Hopkins University in Advanced International Studies. He later worked for the State Department and was posted in Italy where he continues to maintain a residence and an all-Italian collection mirroring his Miami Beach collection.

Wolfson started collecting as a child. He relates, "I collected objects which were parallel to my life, souvenirs of my travels, remembrances of places visited, people met, things encountered." Young Wolfson's keen eye for visual imagery fueled his passion until he totally dedicated himself to the assembly of his collection. As his collection grew, he would send everything to an ornate and impressive fortress called the Washington Storage Company at 1001 Washington Avenue. The "fortress" was an institution of a slowly-disappearing era in Miami Beach history, the era when wealthy families would pack up their entire house-holds at the end of the "season" (usually around Easter) and head back north. The Washington Storage Company would send crews to the departing family's home and empty them of their contents, bringing everything to the storage facility. There, furnishings would be cleaned, repaired, serviced and stored until the family's return the following season. Wolfson took advantage of this convenient facility and sent a growing stream of his purchases there. As the demographics of Miami Beach changed and fewer and fewer families stored their furnishings, Wolfson's collection began to take over. By the 1980s, Wolfson decided to buy the building.

In 1984, Wolfson's collection had grown significant enough to host his first exhibition, a collection of decorative and propaganda arts entitled "Arts in the Service of Ideas and Ideology." The Wolfsonian Institution was founded two years later in 1986. The prime focus of the Wolfsonian was to exhibit Wolfson's collection of decorative and propaganda arts. The collection focused exclusively on the period between 1885 and 1945. These years encompassed the rise of the machine age, mass productions of images and a growing awareness of the persuasive power of art and design. Reasonable prospects for the collection would be items and images from the world fairs and exhibitions, and from railroads, ocean liners and airlines. Political propaganda was also heavily sought after. The vast assemblage of over 120,000 objects also includes glass, ceramics, metalwork, rare books, periodicals, works on paper, textiles, furniture, paintings, prints, industrial and decorative art objects, and ephemera.

All the "isms" of the period between 1885 and 1945 can be found in the Wolfson Collection. Sometimes controversially, this could include Bolshevism, Communism, Nazism, Fascism and more. Wolfson drew large parts of his collection from the English-speaking world (the U.S. and the UK), the Netherlands, the German-speaking countries, the Italians, Czarist and Soviet Russia and the Japanese. In the world of museum collections, there is no parallel to the intellectual focus on design and decorative arts that the Wolfsonian represents.

In 1997, Wolfson announced the donation of the Wolfsonian to Florida International University, the largest gift ever contributed to a public university in Florida. From then on, the Wolfsonian would be known as Wolfsonian-FIU.

Back to the subject of collecting, Wolfson, is still on the prowl. Although it is getting harder to find purchases, it is always a challenge and a thrill to find the right, new and elusive masterpiece. The Wolfsonian-FIU itself buys mainly to support its exhibition and interpretation goals. Some gems of the past include stained glass panels from Irish illustrator Harry Clarke, Mussolini-era railroad station furniture and a door from a Dutch period room integrating themes from a colonial past.

The stained glass panels from Harry Clarke were commissioned by the Irish Free State for the League of Nations. Clarke was a popular Irish illustrator and wished to draw from the rich literary tradition of Ireland to depict a contemporary view of Irish nationality. However, his use of imagery incorporating drunkenness and sexual activity were soundly rejected by the Irish government. Dejected, Clarke put the panels into the family attic. When they were eventually offered for sale, Wolfson snapped them up. Today, they are considered priceless.

In keeping with the fervency which he has displayed throughout his collecting career, Wolfson chased down the Italian workers who in the mid-1980s were removing Mussolini era furniture from the First Class Waiting Room of an Italian train station. His diligence paid off and the furniture is now displayed just outside of the Wolfsonian-FIU's Executive Offices.

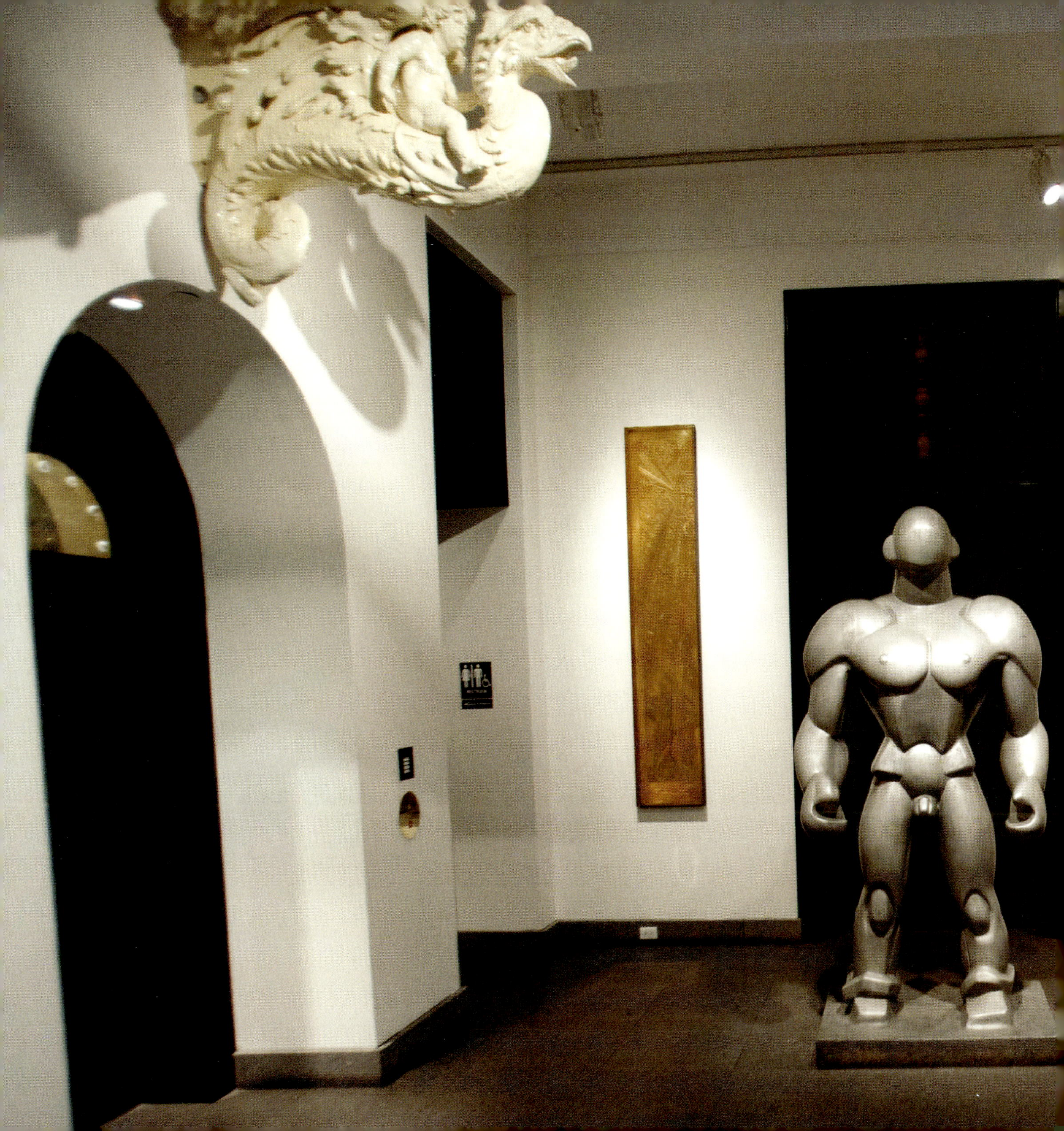

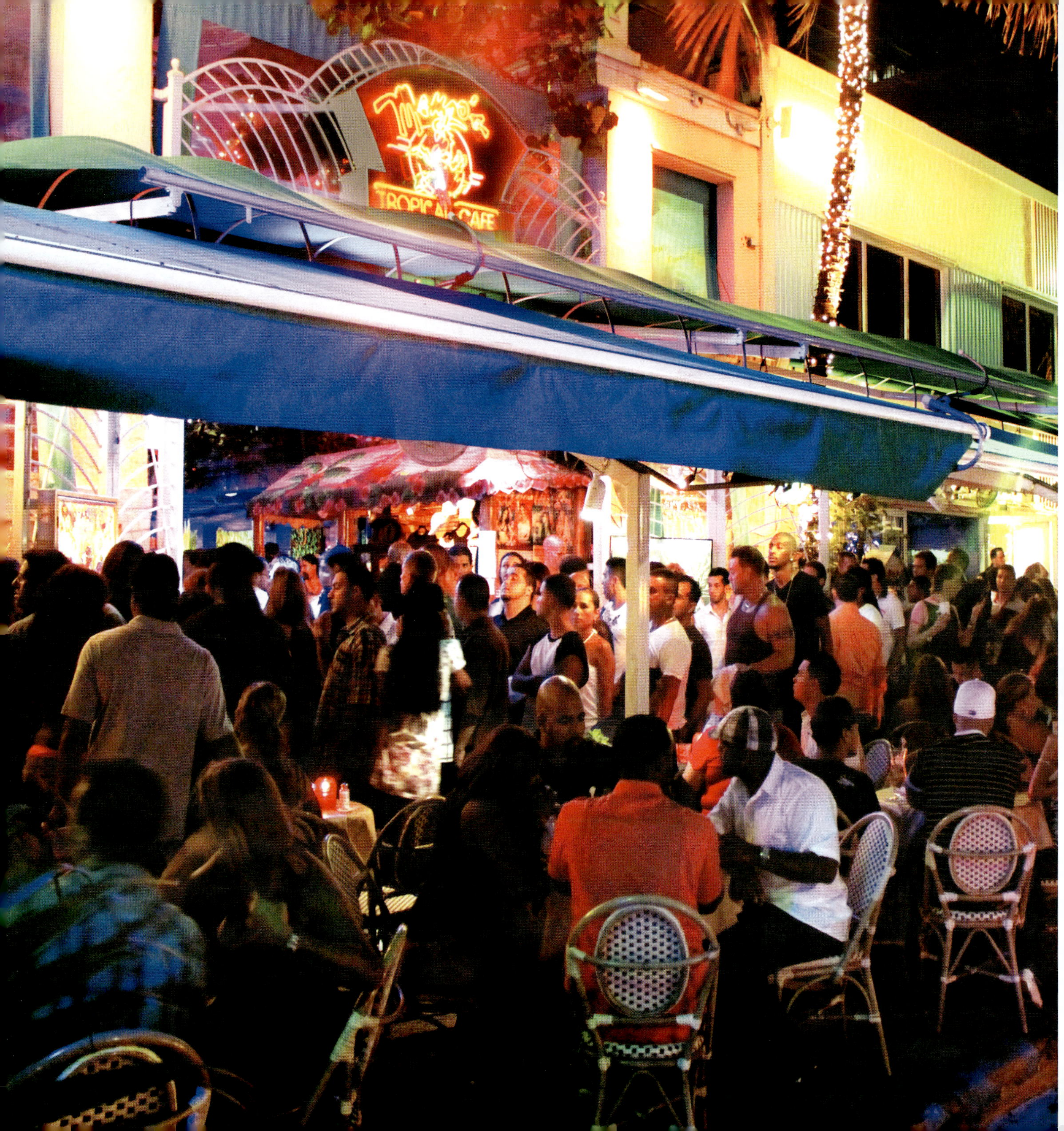
TROPICAL CAFE

Mango's Tropical Cafe

Passing either way on world-famous Ocean Drive, no establishment draws more attention than Mango's Tropical Café. In fact, the place often stops pedestrians, as well as vehicles, right in their tracks. Crowds gather easily on the sidewalk.

Before the rebirth of South Beach, businessman David Wallack owned the first holistic hospice center for elderly people in the area. His tenants ate healthy and well and were kept active and engaged. That was his mission. At the time, David thought that this was what he was going to be doing for the rest of his life. But the beach changed and David's target customers were disappearing.

While taking one of his daily mile-long swims in the Atlantic Ocean which fronts Ocean Drive, David Wallack had a vision. The vision consisted of an international food court, in the middle of which would be a place he would come to call Mango's Tropical Café. The idea for Mango's itself came from David's favorite getaway, the once-tiny Jamaican coastal town of Negril. In those days (the mid 1980s), one had to walk three miles just to get to a telephone in Negril. The only restaurant, which included a night club, in town drew everyone, from guests in dinner jackets to people still in the shorts they put on that morning. David loved the tropical friendliness and informality of the place and this is how he envisioned Mango's would be.

The idea for an international food court and other shops on the first floor, with offices on the second floor, coincided with the city's decision to allow one two-story building per block to be mixed-use. David Wallack's building would be the one. Since banks would not make loans in the area during this time, David took out a mortgage to convert the spaces. When the bank required seven leases, David subdivided the building and started the "high rent" of $45 a square foot with a mandatory 7% percent increase per year. He charged key money for the corner unit and divided up the front shops. The corner unit became a beachwear clothing store called "Wild Things" and the store on the northernmost front of the building is a shoe store, one of over three tenants over 20 years. The center café was broken into three units: the south-side bar area was a pizza and pasta restaurant; the north-side bar was a Mexican restaurant, and the center was Mango's Tropical Café.

With the building's transition taking place, David closed his elderly care business in October of 1990. He did not eject his elderly residents. Mango's opened in March of 1991. When mango season started at the end of summer, he had his remaining elderly residents slicing and bagging the fresh-picked harvest. David had two empty apartments filled with mangos. These produced a couple of thousand pounds of fresh fruit for mango daiquiris.

The early days at Mango's Tropical Café were tough. The building's old elevator was removed and there was no roof over the restaurant. Whenever it rained, guests scrambled under the eaves to try to keep dry. Mostly they would get wet. David budgeted until he could install a canvas top and later a solid skylight roof. Making payroll was likewise difficult. No one would go partners with him in the early days. David was willing to sell 50% percent of the business to an agreeable partner. Even his long-time accountant passed on the opportunity. People were willing to lend but not invest, so David borrowed and paid back various lenders. David smiles and evinces a good deal of entrepreneurial satisfaction when he admits that he's glad that early potential investors turned him down. This enormously profitable business is now all his.

The music in the first years of Mango's was rock and reggae; music David calls "beer music." He would sing with the band and join in on the fun. About four years into the business, Miguel Cruz, who played for Santana, showed up and asked to play. Although he was a wild man who played Afro-Latin jazz, David took the chance, saying "why not?" As soon as Miguel started playing, the girls working at the café, moved by the new infectious rhythm, jumped up onto the bar and began dancing. David looked around and saw how much fun everyone was having and decided that dancing on the bar would be a good thing to do. Miguel Cruz became a friend and Wallack's dancers would eventually dance the tiles right off of the main bar.

Even as beer continued to sell, the cash register started going to Black Label and Bacardi. With this increased source of income, David contracted Miguel Cruz to start playing five days a week.

The sexy and provocative dancing on the bar, the activity that would eventually come to stop traffic on the street and on the sidewalk, began to evolve. David's girlfriend recognized that the dancing was fun but needed to be organized. She realized that the dancing needed to be a "guys and girls experience." She wanted the dance style to be salsa and for it to be carefully choreographed. Routines were established, girls, then guys, then both. The main thrust was heterosexual, although gay clientele were made welcome. Mango's hired servers who were non-dancers and taught them to dance and they hired dancers and taught them to serve. This cross-training became a Mango's innovation. The dancers came from all over the world; Israel, Cuba, Russia, all of South America, and Europe. David refers to his dancers as "great talents" in the longest-running cabaret show in the country.

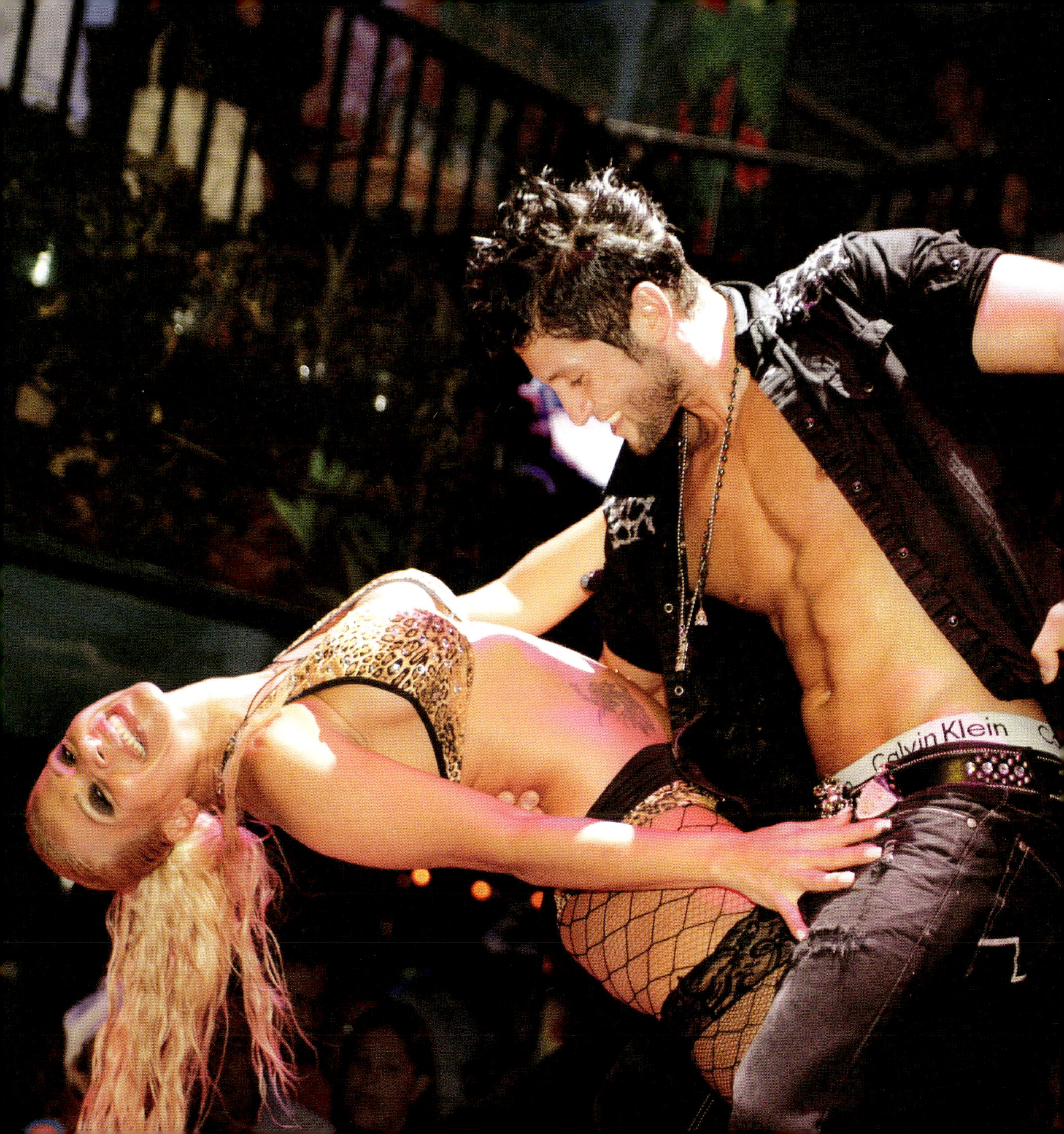
Calvin Klein

BEACH PATROL
HEADQUARTERS

Beach Patrol

The beaches of Miami Beach stretch across eight and a half miles. It is the responsibility of the Beach Patrol to keep people from drowning in the ocean that fronts the beach. Twenty-nine Lifeguard Stations have been erected to provide shelter for the more than 100 lifeguards who are part of the Beach Patrol. The changed stands are a result of the widespread destruction of Miami Beach's former lifeguard stands during Hurricane Andrew in 1992. That hurricane was one of the most destructive in history.

Architect William Lane and Artist Kenny Scharf collaborated to create a group of highly decorative, broadly individualistic entries into Miami Beach architecture. Using images like lighthouses and tiny, rounded spaceships and employing colors like deep aqua, yellow, lavender and bright pink, the lighthouses came to define the image of Miami Beach to the world. Even after a series of hurricanes in 2005 took some of the beloved stands away, new marvelously creative stands have taken their place.

The lifeguard stands are the domain of a tight cadre of professionals called the Miami Beach Ocean Rescue Division (Part of the Miami Beach Fire Department) more colloquially, they are known as the "Beach Patrol." Their headquarters is the 1939, Robert Taylor-designed art deco gem facing the beach at 10th and Ocean. This architectural masterpiece was designed to resemble the bridge of a 1930s era ocean liner.

Much of the work of a lifeguard is preventative, Miami Beach has some notorious rip currents and when those currents strike, the race to save lives is on. The lifeguards on the Beach Patrol need to be strong enough to pull two or three people from the rip currents by themselves. There is a lighter side to their work. They know what is happening on the beach and help with lost children and insect bites as well as other minor emergencies.

An innovation that came to play an important role in the development of the modern Beach Patrol was the introduction of 4-wheeled ATV's (All Terrain Vehicles). This allows for a quick response to emergencies.

Owing to the fact that the Lifeguard stands have been in place since the mid 1990s, they have experienced a lot of wear and tear from the wind and salt air. Newly designed stations are replacing the old ones by Miami Beach's Centennial in 2015, designed by the same architect.

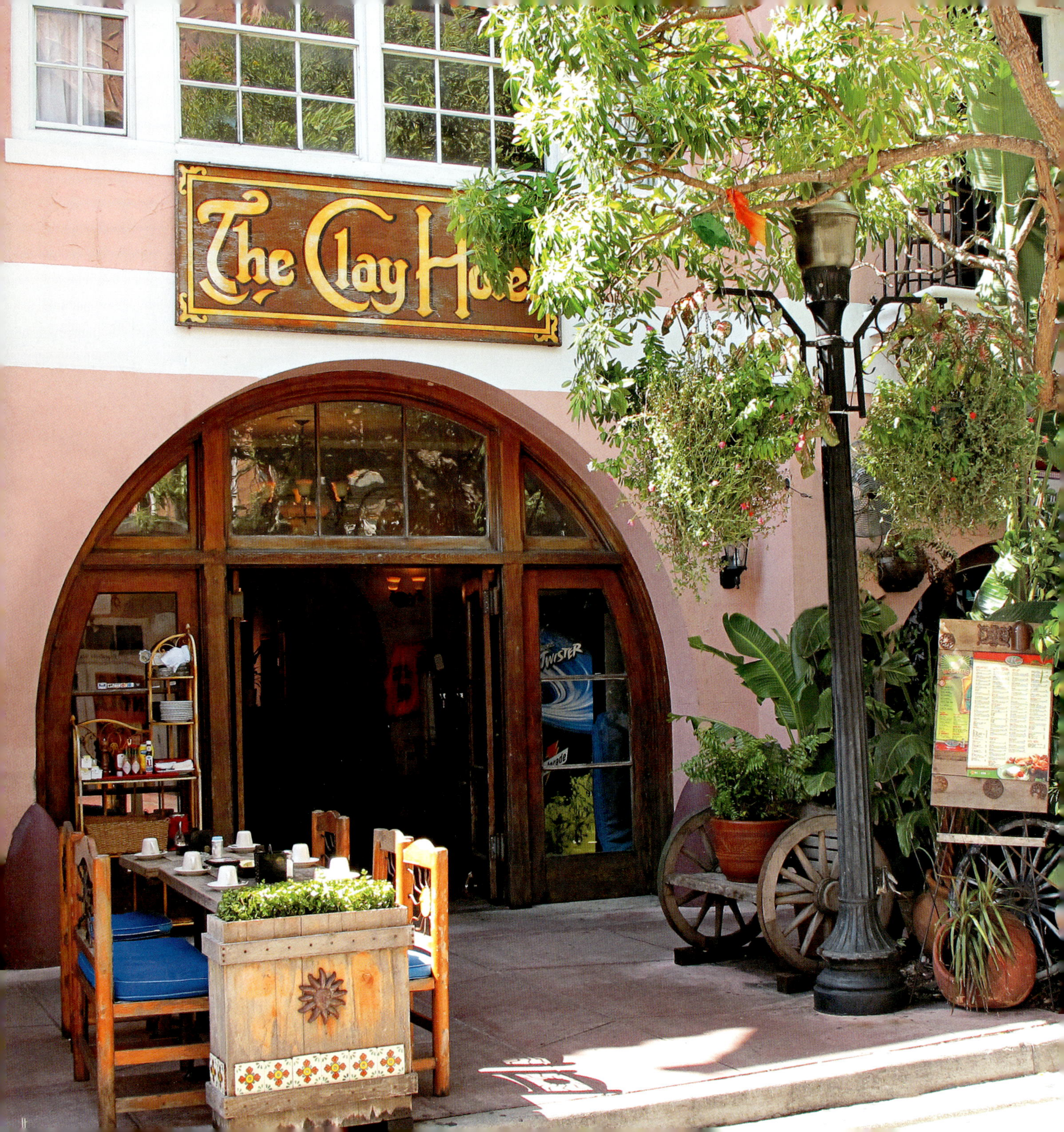
The Clay
TWISTER

Española Way

Newton B.T. Roney, was one of the major developers in Miami Beach and was often the subject of newspaper articles due to daring and adventurous activities. For reporters to remember the sequence of the initials in his name he was privately referred to as "Newton Bath Tub".

Roney first came to Miami Beach in 1909 from Camden, New Jersey, and by 1918, he became a full-time resident. By 1925, during the Florida land boom, he was one of the largest land-owners. He built the Roney Plaza, a luxurious and popular oceanfront hotel, on 23rd Street; which opened in 1925.

What was missing in Miami Beach, he believed, was an area where artists, and those people interested in art, could congregate, such as existed in Greenwich Village, New York, or the Left-bank in Paris. He saw an opportunity to create such an artistic colony on the property that was originally owned by the Lummus Brothers. The area became known as Española Way, located between 14th and 15th Streets and Washington Avenue.

Roney's architect was Robert A. Taylor. Together Roney and Taylor decided on a Spanish theme for this artists' colony, which would be modeled after towns on the Spanish Coast. They planned the construction of 16 buildings including two fifty-room hotels, apartment buildings and shops. It was estimated to cost $1,500,000. During the 1920s the shops on Española Way were designed to meet the desires of the wealthy people. There were antique stores, rare book stores, shops where you could buy jewelry, designer clothes; and it was aimed to "set the style for Paris," not emulate it.

While the expectation was for a great and thriving artists' colony to develop, artists did not seem to adopt this street as their own. Maybe it was too well designed, or too planned. During this time, crime escalated, brothels opened, and the area went into general decline. Whatever the reason, the area appealed more to the wild crowd than to artists and became home to bookies, and boot-leggers.

Soldiers took over during WWII as the hotels in Miami Beach were requisitioned for military use. After the war, dance studios predominated and it is here where 18 year old Desi Arnaz appeared at a local restaurant and and began the craze for Latin music.

Most of South Beach went into decline during the 1970s and Española Way was part of the down-fall. Barbara Polansky, was so enthralled by the area that she purchased the entire south side of Española Way and through her efforts brought it back to become a vibrant, prosperous area. It was Polansky who fielded the interest of a production designer for a new television series to be called "Miami Vice." Española Way, with its newly painted peach streetscape would go on to become the permanent backdrop for the series.

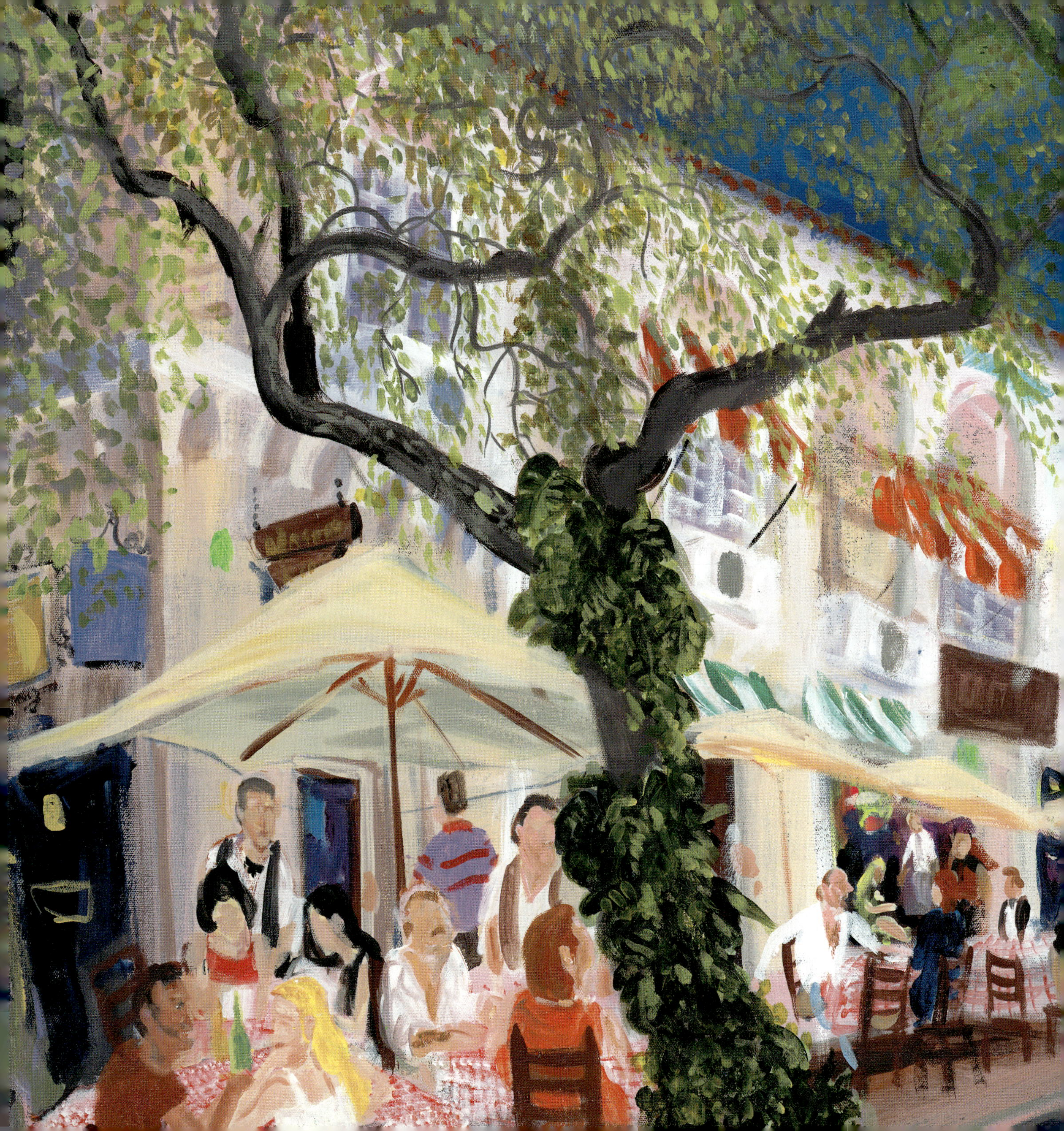

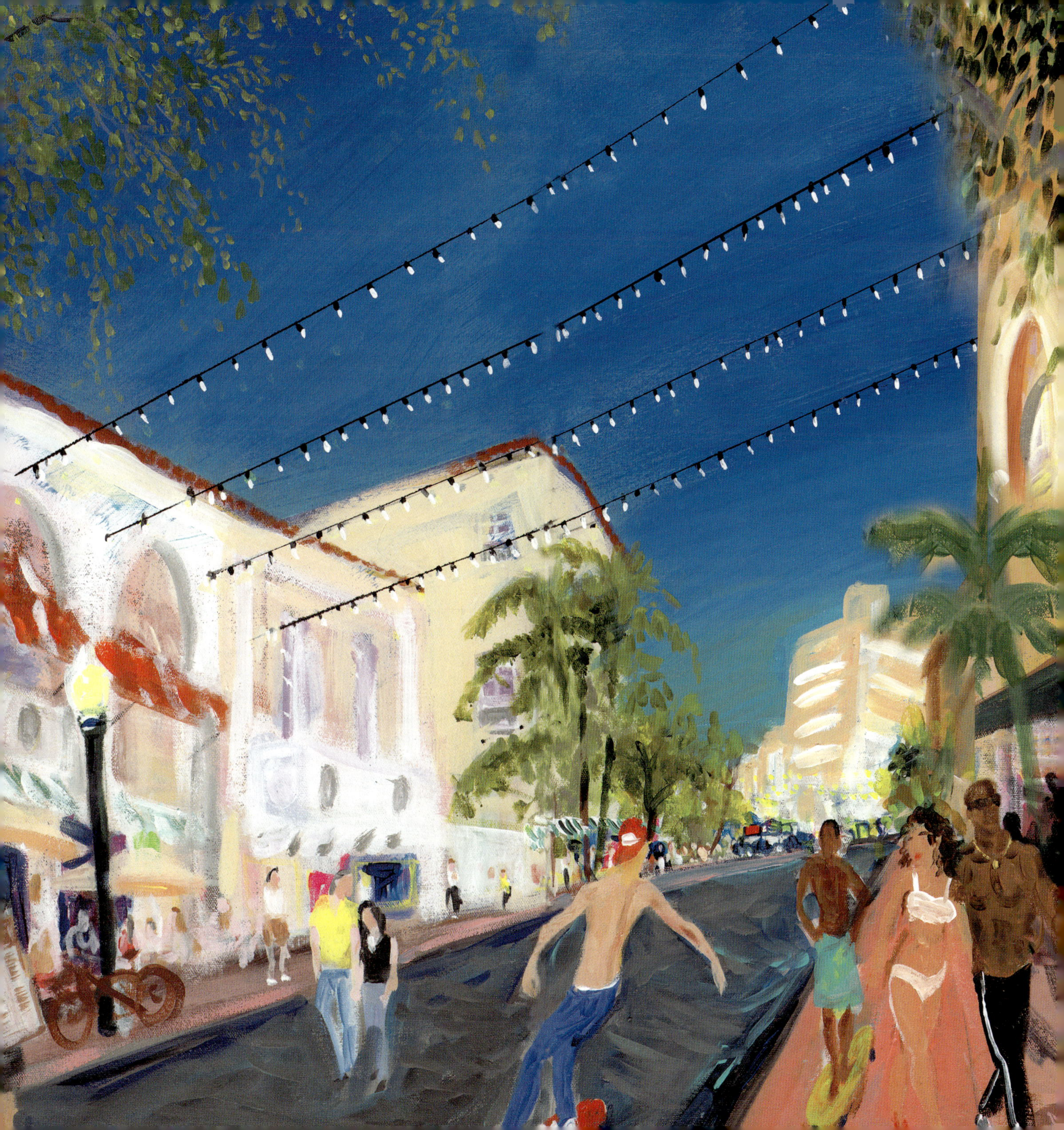

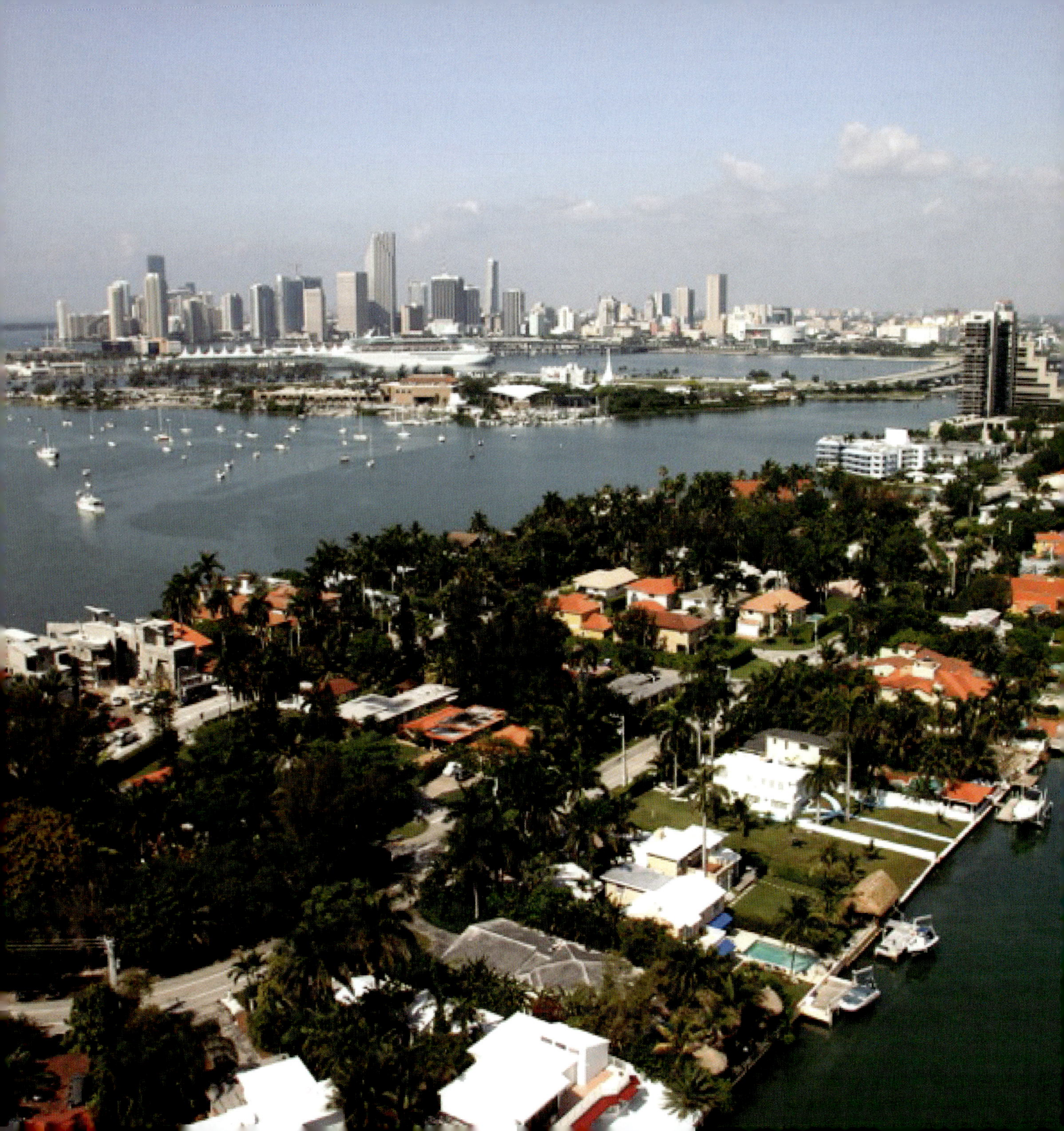

Venetian Isles

John Collins, began farming in Miami Beach in the late 1800s. His desire to get his products to market efficiently, encouraged him to build a bridge to connect Miami Beach to the City of Miami. Until then the only way to ship products from the City to the Beach was by ferry.

With the assistance of his son-in-law, Thomas Pancoast and an investment from Carl Fisher, Collins built a bridge of 2.5 miles that was the longest wooden bridge in the world. The bridge was opened in 1913.

The incredible land boom that occurred in the twenties, led to the desire to develop more acreage. The Biscayne Bay Improvement Company began selling lots neighboring the Collins Bridge, that were underwater, with the promise that seawalls, roads and utilities would be provided.

The process known as "island building" created a chain of six man-made islands. Four of these islands are part of Miami Beach, while two are part of the City of Miami. The islands were created by a dredging process from the Bay and soil from Government Cut. The six islands are Belle Isle, which was partly natural but was enhanced by land-fill, Rivo Alto Island, DeLido Island, San Marino Island and San Marco Island.

Belle Isle was the only one of the Venetian Isles to have a natural foundation. Belle Isle was a rough mangrove hammock situated in Biscayne Bay. When John Collins built his canal to transport produce from Miami Beach to the City of Miami, much of the sand that had been dredged was deposited around the hammock. The land mass of Belle Isle was enhanced. The Collins bridge crossed over this land and enabled the building of a shorter bridge.

Belle Isle became an enclave for wealthy people and it was near this island that Fisher created Speed Boat races in the Biscayne Bay for the enjoyment of his friends.

In 1926, the Collins Bridge was replaced by the Venetian Causeway. At the time there was one island, Bull Island that existed between the mainland and the Beach. The name was changed from Bull Island to Belle Isle.

In the 1920s and 1930s Belle Isle was the most well-known of the Venetian Isles. J.C. Penney had purchased a home there in 1921. He had invited President Herbert Hoover to vacation at his home in 1929. This brought a great deal of news coverage to the island.

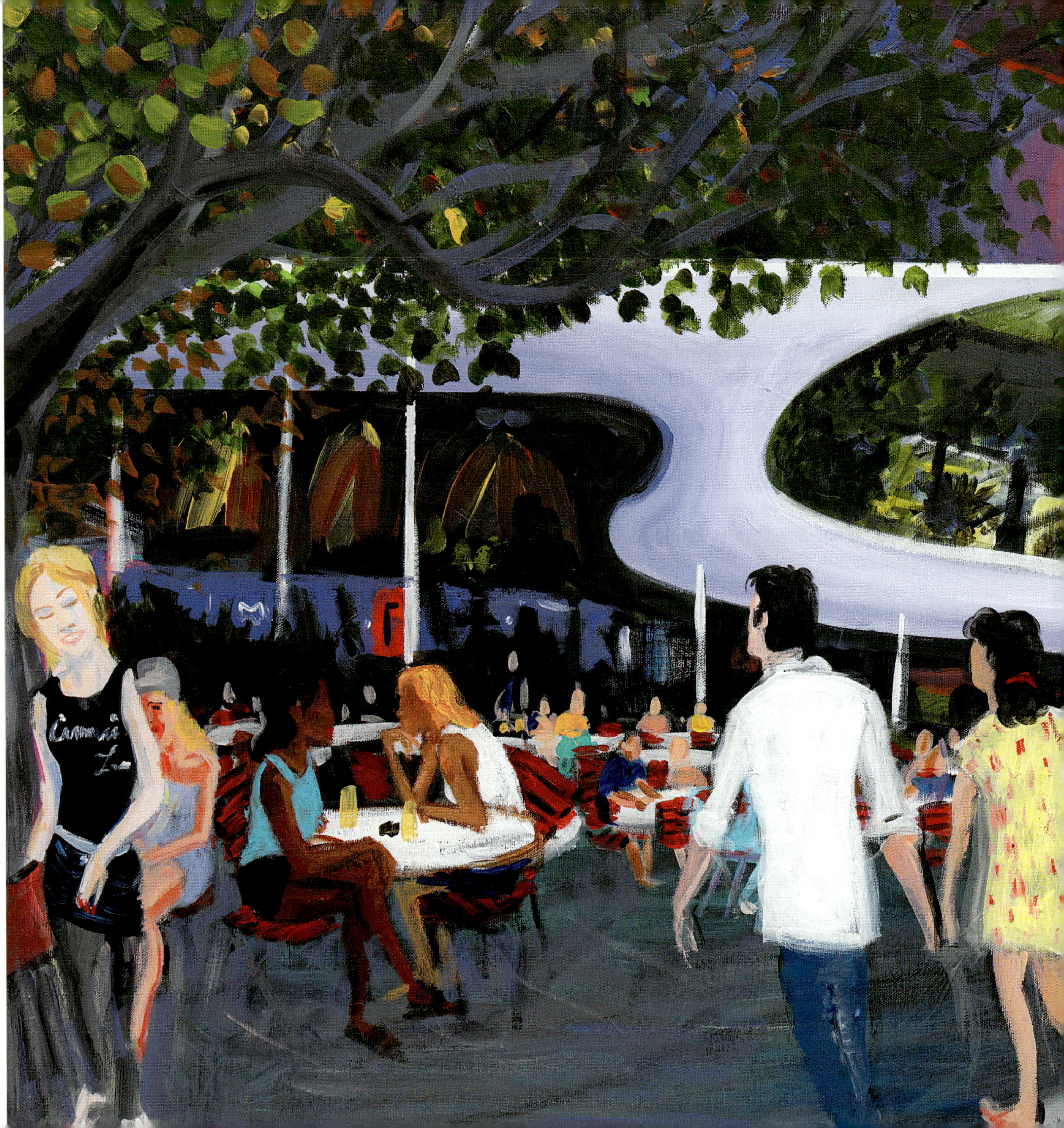

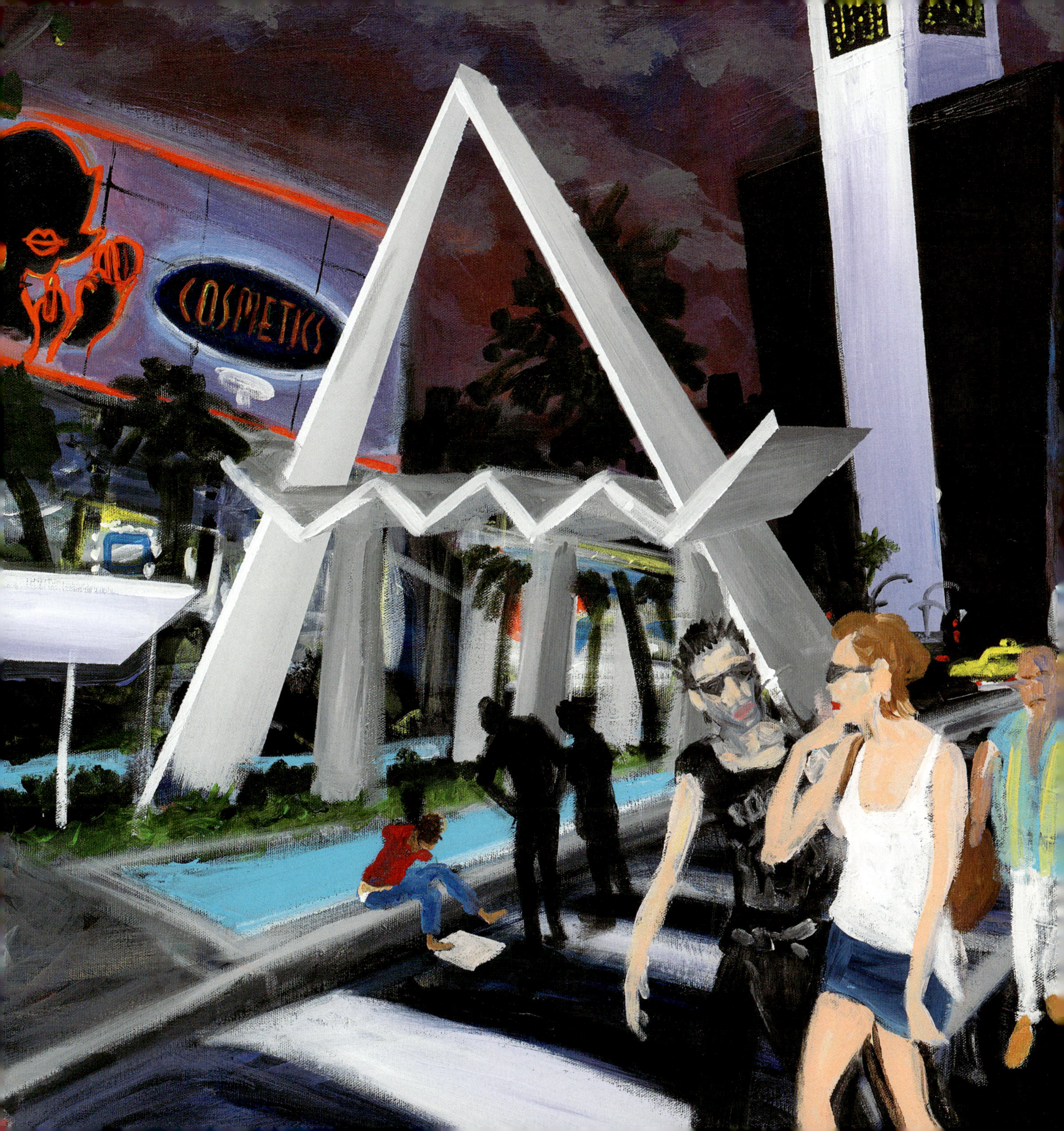
COSMETICS

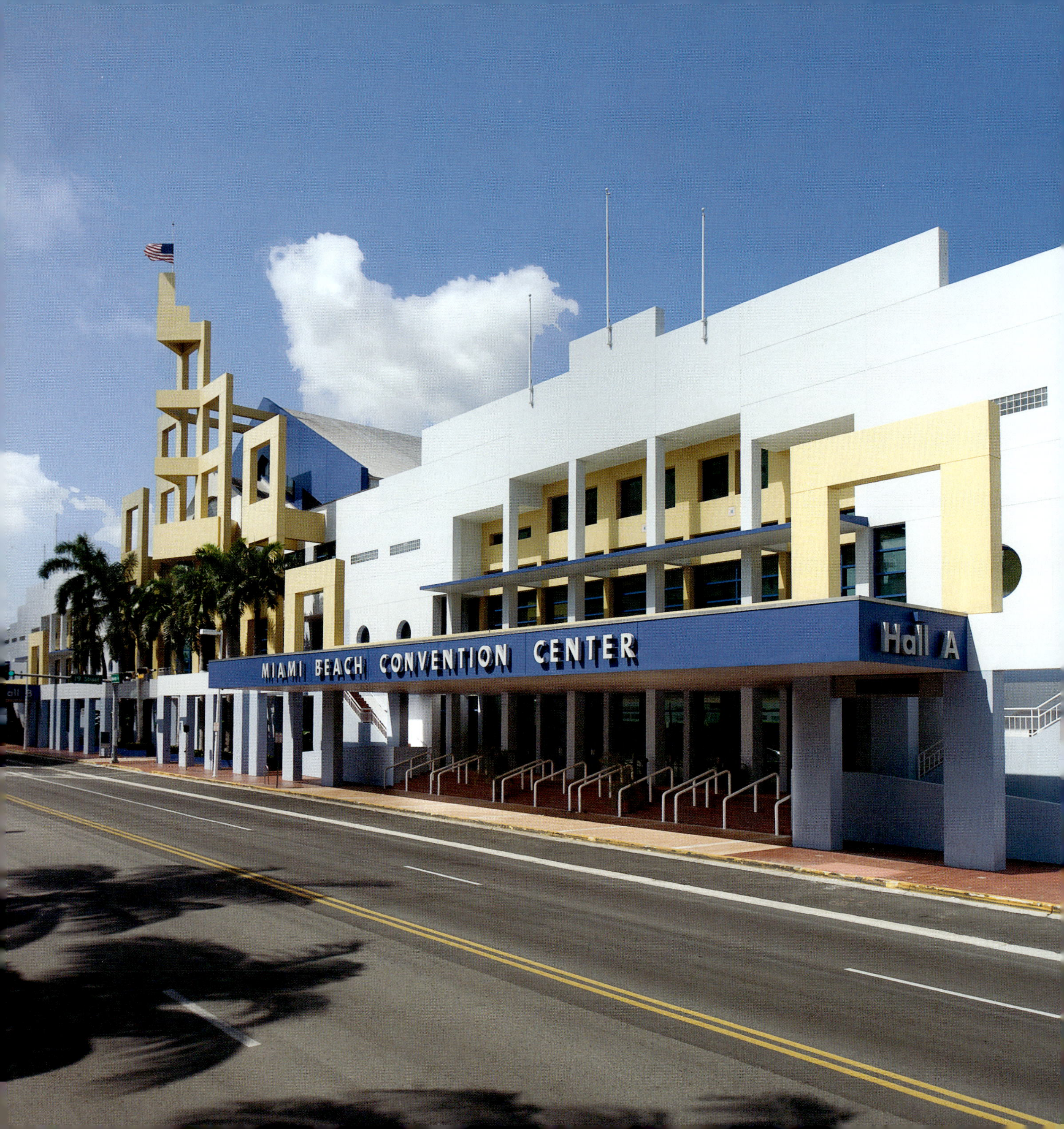
MIAMI BEACH CONVENTION CENTER
Hall A

Miami Beach Convention Center

At 100,000 square feet the Miami Beach Convention Center was the biggest meeting venue in the Southeast in the 1950s. Connected by a bridge to the Miami Beach Auditorium, the Convention Center headlined some of the largest gatherings in the country. From the mid-1960s to the early 1970s, Miami Beach was in the national spotlight. Much of the attention focused on activities at the Convention Center.

Two things happened in 1964 that put the Convention Center in the spotlight. The first thing was the decision by Jackie Gleason to move his wildly popular show to Miami Beach Auditorium, (part of the Convention Center complex) from New York. After upgrades, the auditorium would become known as the Jackie Gleason Theater. Everyone came down from New York on the "Jackie Gleason Express". The writers, dancers and singers that followed Jackie became part of the local community.

The second banner event in 1964, that gained world attention, was the Clay-Liston Prize Fight. Sonny Liston was World Champion. Cassius Clay (who had not yet made the identity transition to Mohammad Ali) was the pugnacious, super-charged challenger. The old Convention Center facility added another building, doubling the square footage to 200,000 square feet. The addition helped snag the 1968 Republican Convention. Four years later, in 1972, Miami Beach got both the Democratic and the Republican national conventions.

By the early 1980s, there was a definite consensus that the Convention Center needed to be enlarged. The idea was postulated, that if the Convention Center was expanded, someone would build a major convention hotel. In 1985, a tax was passed that would fund the addition of two more halls, bringing the Center's footprint to four halls, encompassing over one million square feet. In January of 1989, two new halls were opened and the following year, the two older halls were renovated. Still, there was no new hotel on the horizon.

The Miami Beach Chamber of Commerce, formed a committee to get a new hotel built. The City got involved, passed a 1% bed tax and issued an RFP (Request for Proposal) for a new hotel. The beachfront site where the New York and Sands Hotels stood was selected and the hotels came down overnight. Eight companies responded to the RFP. The Loews Hotel was selected, broke ground in 1996 and opened in 1998.

Perhaps, the most significant event of all, with the greatest impact for the City of Miami Beach is the art fair known as Art Basel. Taking place every December, since 2002 is an event that brings together the most significant collection of art from more than 250 galleries, from five continents. It has been called "the biggest art happening on the planet".

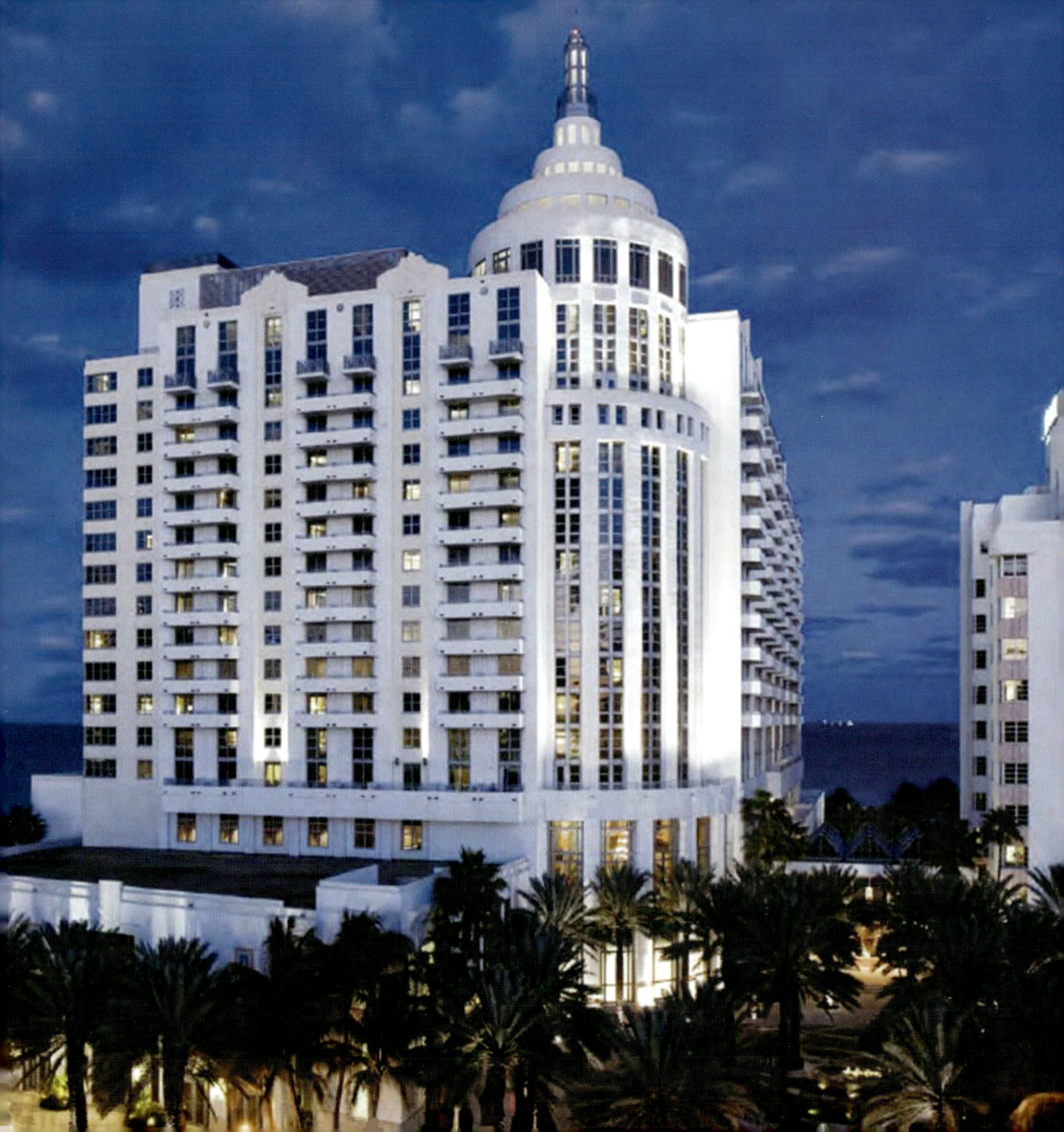

Loews / St. Moritz Hotel

When the Miami Beach Convention Center began to receive many activities it became evident that a major hotel was needed to compete with other cities with large convention facilities. To prepare for the new hotel, the City of Miami Beach purchased a group of aging oceanfront hotels at 16th Street and Collins Avenue. These were the Sands, the New Yorker and the St. Moritz. The Sands and New Yorker came down overnight. The St. Moritz was spared with the aim of incorporating it into the new hotel project.

The City of Miami put out an RFP (Request for Proposal) to the hotel community. Nine hotel companies were in the final competition to receive the support of the City to build the hotel. Each of the nine was given an hour to make a formal presentation before the City Commission and a public audience of about four hundred people. Jonathan Tisch's family owned a theater chain and several successful hotels. The family decided to submit a proposal to build the convention hotel.

Jonathan Tisch, who headed up the effort on behalf of his family and Loews Corporation, remembers the pressure. He had to oversee a great design and convince the City Commission and the public and the management of his own company of the merits of his proposal. He had the unenviable position of being first to make his presentation. For 55 minutes he made a hard-driving pitch. Then he took a great risk. He decided to copy an idea that David Letterman had used. Letterman had sent his mother to interview people at the Winter Olympics. Tisch decided to film his mother interviewing people on the streets of Miami Beach. He couldn't work up the courage to approach his mother. Instead, he dressed in drag, as his mother, and did the filming. This segment would take up the last five minutes of his presentation. As the film started rolling, no one laughed for the first 30 seconds. Suddenly, the audience realized the woman doing the interviewing was Jonathan in drag and they began howling with laughter. Tisch believes that this moment of levity and creativity helped win the contract.

Tisch embarked on a daily ritual of work and worry. Construction started in 1997 and was completed Christmas Eve 1999. The restoration of the St. Moritz Hotel was incorporated into the hotel complex.

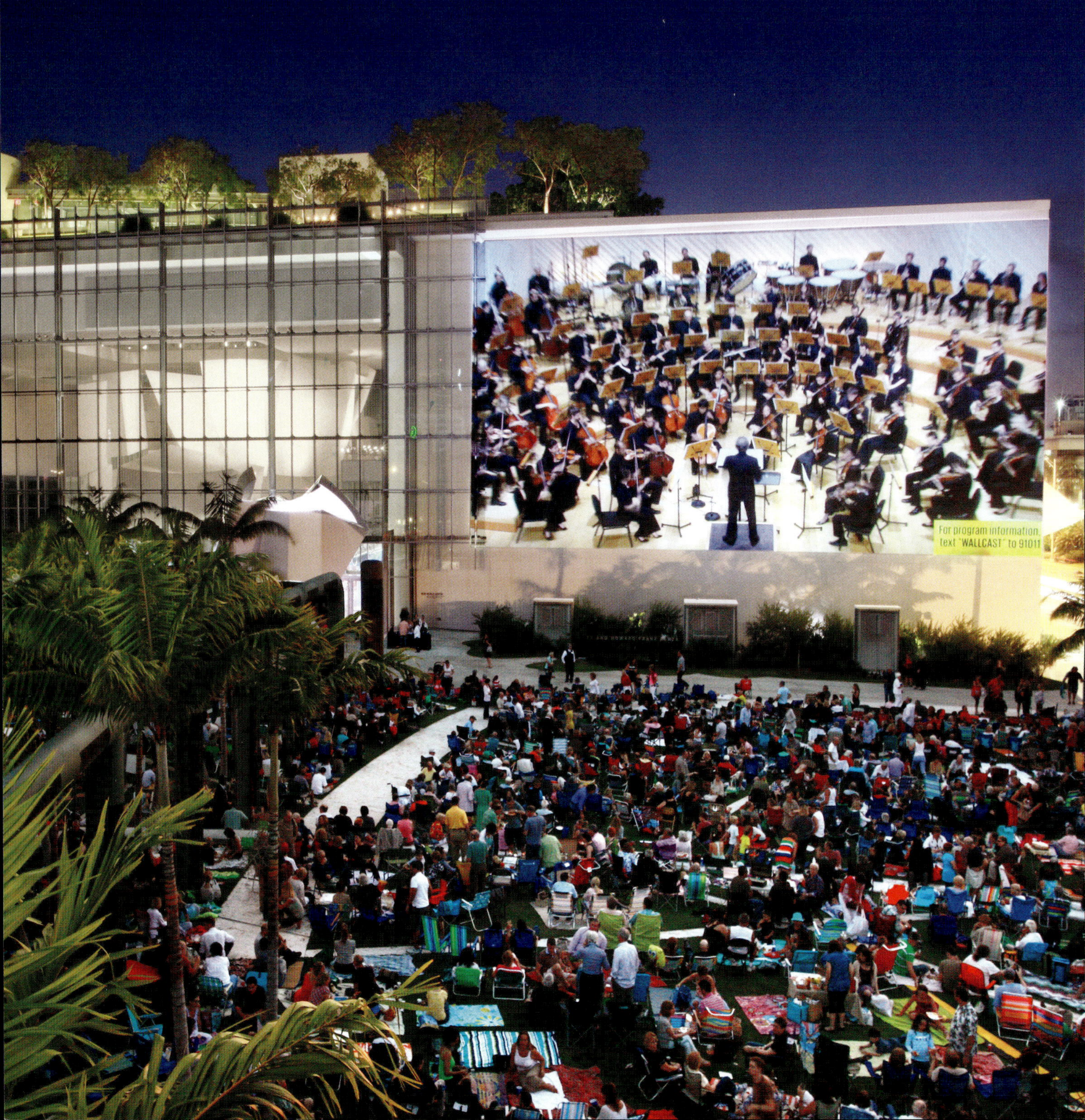
For program information,
text "WALLCAST" to 91011

New World Symphony

On January 25, 2011 the New World Symphony moved into its very own home, in a spectacular building designed by world famous architect, Frank Gehry. Michael Tilson Thomas is the person behind the great achievement of this monumental building. It has been his dream to encourage the appreciation of classical music and he has devoted his life's work as a conductor, composer and teacher to see that great classical music endures and is cherished by generations to come.

At age three, when most children are learning the alphabet, Thomas was already taking piano lessons. He comes from a musical family going back to his grandparents, who were famous in the Yiddish Theater in New York City. He was raised in Hollywood, California in an atmosphere surrounded by friends and relatives in a stimulating cultural environment.

Thomas founded the New World Symphony in 1987, in order to provide the opportunity for young gifted musicians to develop leadership skills so that they would be prepared to assume positions in ensembles and orchestras any place in the world. This was his way of ensuring that there would be a cadre of qualified people to carry on the important work to guarantee that great music in the classical tradition would survive. It is said that more than half of the musicians in orchestras and ensembles in the world today were trained by the New World Symphony.

Ted Arison, founder of Carnival Cruise Lines, and his wife Lin, lovers of classical music were the people who shared Thomas' dream of creating an institution dedicated to nurturing the talents of young musicians and providing an atmosphere where they could flourish. To that end, the Arisons provided funding for outstanding graduates of conservatories to study and hone their talents under the guidance of Thomas. Housing was provided for students and in November, 1987 about 55 students moved into the old Plymouth Hotel, in South Beach, to share the residence with about twenty-five elderly residents.

The new building is spectacular. It is set behind a soaring, 80-foot high glass wall, leading to an atrium with geometric forms and an undulating, green-tinted titanium canopy. The outside of the building, features a 7,000 square-foot projection wall which enables live transmission of concerts from within the building. The wall features an ever-changing video mural when not projecting performances from inside. A public park is located to the east of the building so that the great performances can be shared by the many tourists and residents who frequent Lincoln Road.

The collaboration of two American artistic icons, Michael Tilson Thomas and Frank Gehry, has resulted in a unique cultural treasure which enhances South Beach immeasurably.

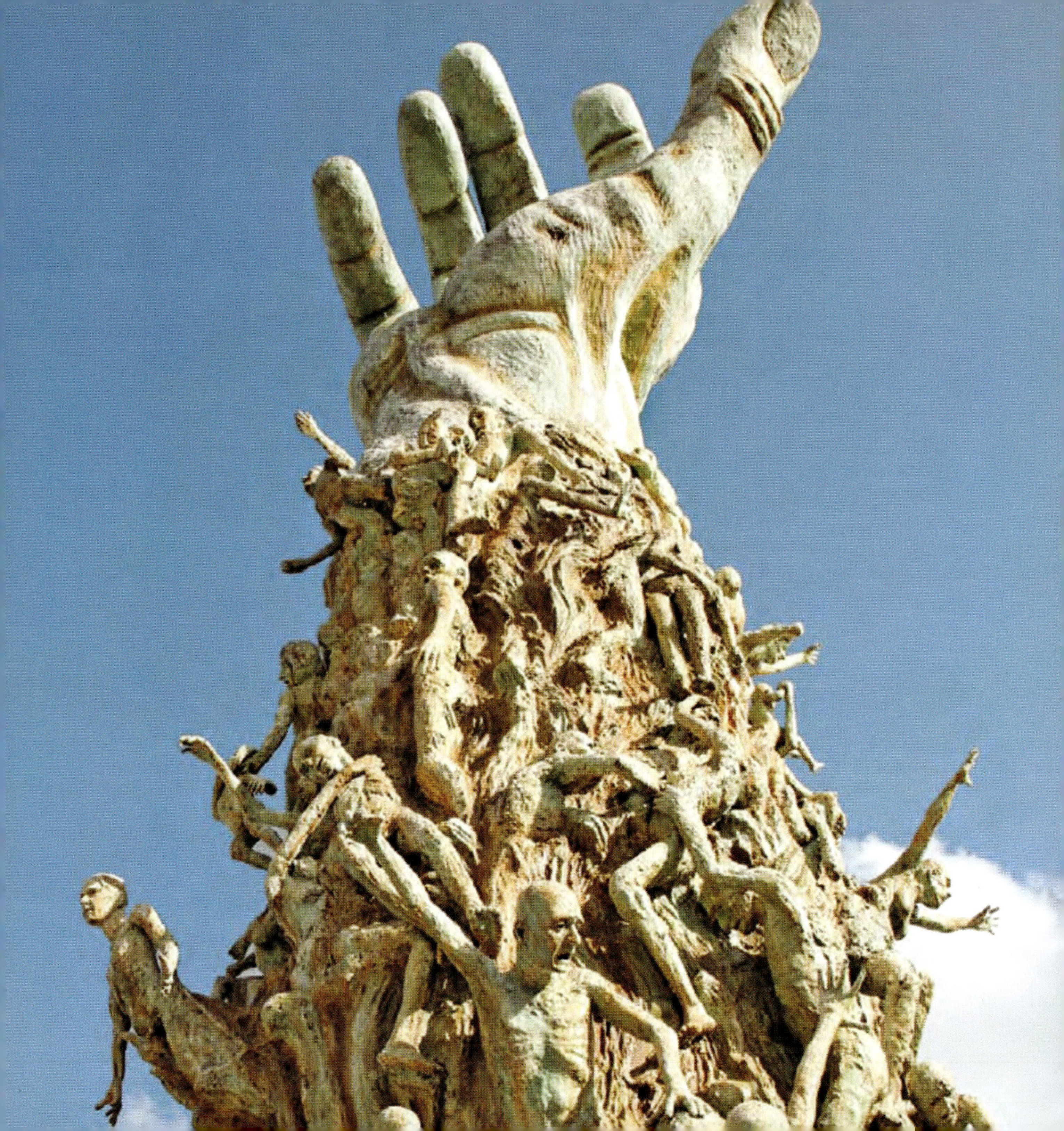

Holocaust Memorial

The most jarring image in South Beach is of a human arm reaching into the heavens, its tattooed number clearly visible, emaciated figures climbing upon it, trying to escape some horrific destiny.

As survivors of the holocaust started to get older, their bodies, savaged years earlier by concentration camp life, many were ill-prepared to handle the cold winters of the American northeast. Some retired to South Beach for the warm weather and the close-knit urban fabric that it offered. With a concentration of survivors in one place, the idea of a holocaust memorial materialized. At the time, there were no other holocaust memorials in the U.S. In fact, there was only one other in the entire world, which was Yad Vashem in Jerusalem. The South Beach memorial would be both groundbreaking and symbolic.

A committee, led by Norman Braman, a local automobile dealer, was formed to advance the holocaust memorial project. In 1980, the committee approached Ken Treister, an accomplished author, architect, painter, sculptor and photographer. Besides asking him to join the committee, they also asked him to design the memorial itself. Ken agreed to take on the project under two conditions: one, that he had complete artistic freedom, and two, that the memorial had to be strong and forceful. Braman gave a third condition of his own: stay within budget.

Staying within budget was challenging. After completing the original design sketches, Treister, along with Braman, approached George Segal, a sculptor noted for his realistic cast figures. Meanwhile the committee worked on selecting an appropriate site for the memorial. One particular location showed a lot of promise. The site in question had some old homes that had just been torn down. Additionally, it was only a stone's throw away from the Miami Beach Convention Center, assuring a steady stream of potential visitors. It backed up to a local garden club, a remaining vestige of Miami Beach's Gentile community, a place where the ladies socialized. Who would have guessed the controversy that such an ideal site would bring. But controversial it was! Why controversy? The garden club didn't want a monument to such an ugly chapter in human history at its back door. Therefore, a committee was formed to oppose the memorial. The battle lines were drawn: the garden club committee versus thousands of holocaust survivors. The fight for the memorial was about to get ugly.

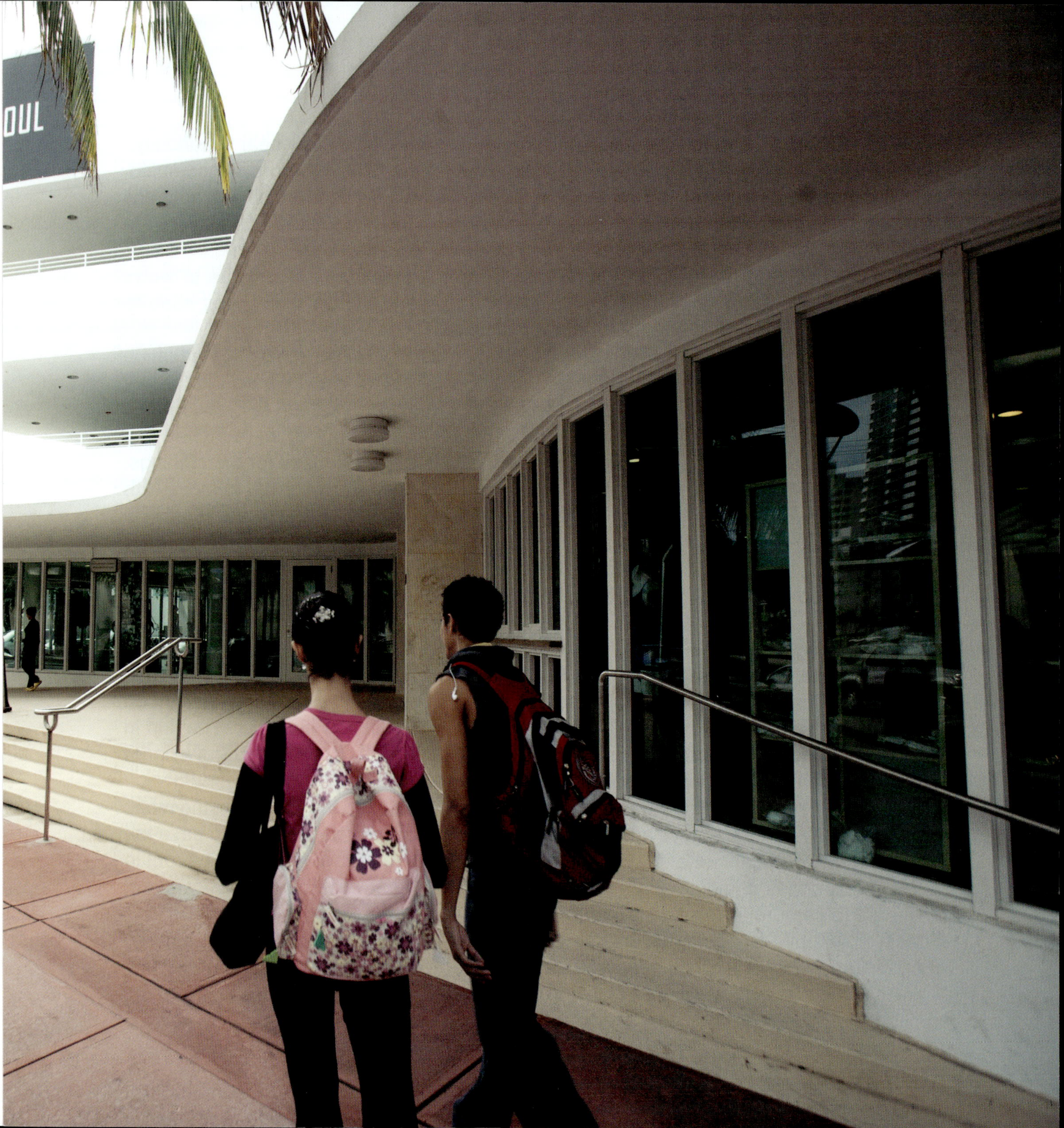
OUL

Miami City Ballet

The Miami City Ballet resides in a beautiful 60,000 square foot building in the arts district on the northernmost edge of South Beach. Its 60-by-40-foot studios with 22 foot ceilings offer an optimal environment for the ballet company's 55 dancers. The themes of movement, light, sand and water are worked artfully into the motifs of the floor and the building. There is an overall influence of art deco incorporated into the architecture. Although inspiring, beautiful and hard-won, all of these features are simply the façade. The "spirit" of the ballet company takes us back to the 1980s and a far scrappier beginning.

No history of the Miami City Ballet can begin without introducing Edward Villella. Villella grew up in Queens, New York. With his mother, he used to accompany his sister to her ballet classes. With his natural energy he would jump around the room. The teacher made a demand. If you are going to leap around here you must go to the bar and participate. He soon emerged as the best student in the class. At the age of ten he was enrolled in the School of American Ballet. He later attended the New York Maritime College where he became a welterweight boxing champion and lettered in Baseball.

The New York Italian kid who used his boxing skills to defend his passion for ballet dancing set world records for his vertical leaps. When his stellar dancing career came to its natural conclusion, Villella had some decisions to make. He wanted to remain in the dynamic world of ballet, but now he had to move from dance to the business of managing a ballet dance company.

Although he was well trained as a dancer, Villella relates that a good dancer does not equal a good director. So, he set off to self-learn the business. The ballet's first home was a storefront on Lincoln Road, in 1985. The lonely, largely abandoned thoroughfare had once epitomized wealth and sophistication on Miami Beach. Although the joke at the time was that you could shoot a cannon on Lincoln Road and not hit anyone, the storefront location was to be an iconic and popular one. As Miami Beach in general, and Lincoln Road in particular started to come back to life, people on their lunch breaks would watch the ballet dancers practice from their outside vantage point of the sidewalk. In 1987, the ballet company had a one million dollar budget, essentially a start-up operation. There were junkies and frequent incidents of street crime on Lincoln Road.

From the very beginning, Edward Villella set an ambitious course for the Miami City

Ballet. He toured as a startup company, even performing at the New York City Ballet. He chose a company of 55 dancers because he could manage 55 dancers without going crazy and because he could "teach" 55 dancers and because that's how many can fit in a single room.

Holding continuous auditions, Villella built a pure repertoire company, not a company of stars. Just to add one more caveat, Edward Villella does not subscribe to the "flavor of the month" club. He didn't jump on bandwagons when it comes to dance. This serious, mature approach to building a cultural institution gathered ambitious, young dancers from nations all over the world (Russia, China, Cuba, etc.). Villella's proudest accomplishment has been the acquisition of the new building in 2000.

Another great occasion occurred for the ballet in 2012 when it received thunderous standing ovations in Paris from over-flow crowds. Villella was thrilled. "We are operating at the highest levels," he said.

But when he returned home it was to devastating news; a huge financial crisis. The ballet had over 2 million dollars in debt. The board was at odds with Villella; claiming he was not adhering to budgetary requirements. Villella abruptly resigned and a new artistic director, Lourdes Lopez replaced him.

Lopez was born in Havana Cuba in 1958. Her family left Cuba for Miami, where she grew up. As a child her leg muscles were weak and her doctor recommended that she have a strenuous physical activity. Her mother took her to ballet class, and that started Lopez's love of the dance. By eleven she was enrolled at the School of American Ballet. At sixteen, she was a member of the corps de ballet of the New York City Ballet. She has had a long career in many aspects of performing, teaching and as a dance company administrator.

Lopez says that she does not want the Miami City Ballet to become like a museum so to that end she will be adding edgier works to the core.

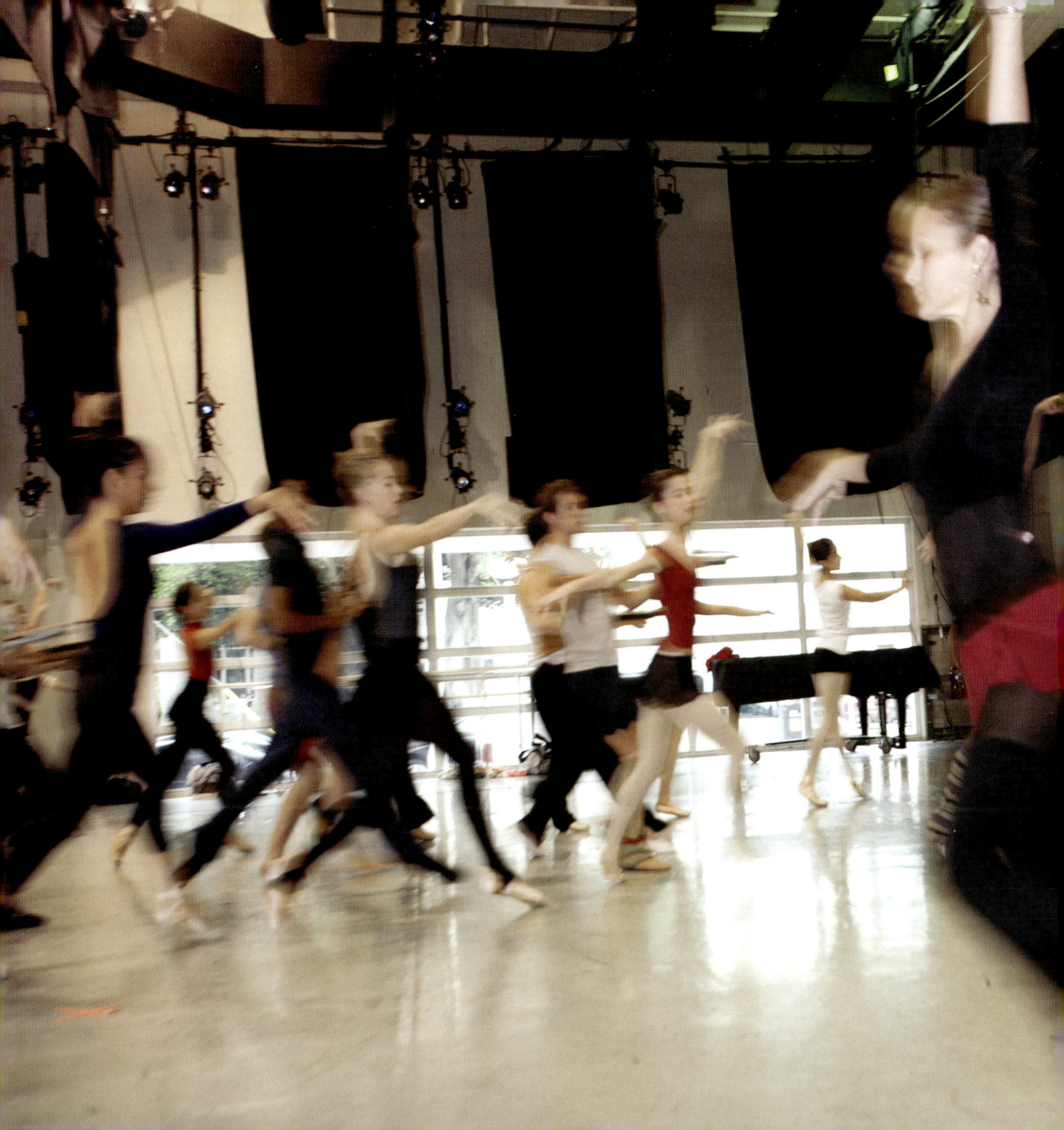

Mid Beach

The Fontainebleau and Eden Roc Hotels
41st Street (Arthur Godfrey Road)
Normandy Isles/The Vendome Fountain
LaGorce Island

Mid Beach, starting at Dade Boulevard to the south and connecting with 23rd Street to the east, climbs all the way to 63rd Street mid-island. This expansive section of Miami Beach takes in many upscale residential neighborhoods including Bayshore, La Gorce Country Club, Pine Tree Drive and the mansions along Indian Creek. It also encompasses miles of oceanfront condominiums and hotel resorts. Mid Beach is home to the internationally known Fontainebleau and Eden Roc resort hotels. The area has two well known golf courses; the beautiful, public, Miami Beach Golf Club and the exclusive, private, LaGorce Country Club.

Hosting at least a dozen local synagogues, the Mid Beach area has a thriving, multi-congregational Jewish community alongside large populations of Latinos, Europeans and other mainstream American residents. Mid Beach is also home to the City of Miami Beach's only full-scale hospital, the Mount Sinai Medical Center.

The last five years have witnessed dramatic restoration and redevelopment of the ocean-facing hotels from 23rd Street to 43rd Street, just below the Fontainebleau Hotel and the area just north of the 5900 block of Collins Avenue. Mid Beach is well built-out and up-to-date. Save for the occasional mansion teardown and redo, the Mid Beach area is not likely to see much more extensive change in the near future.

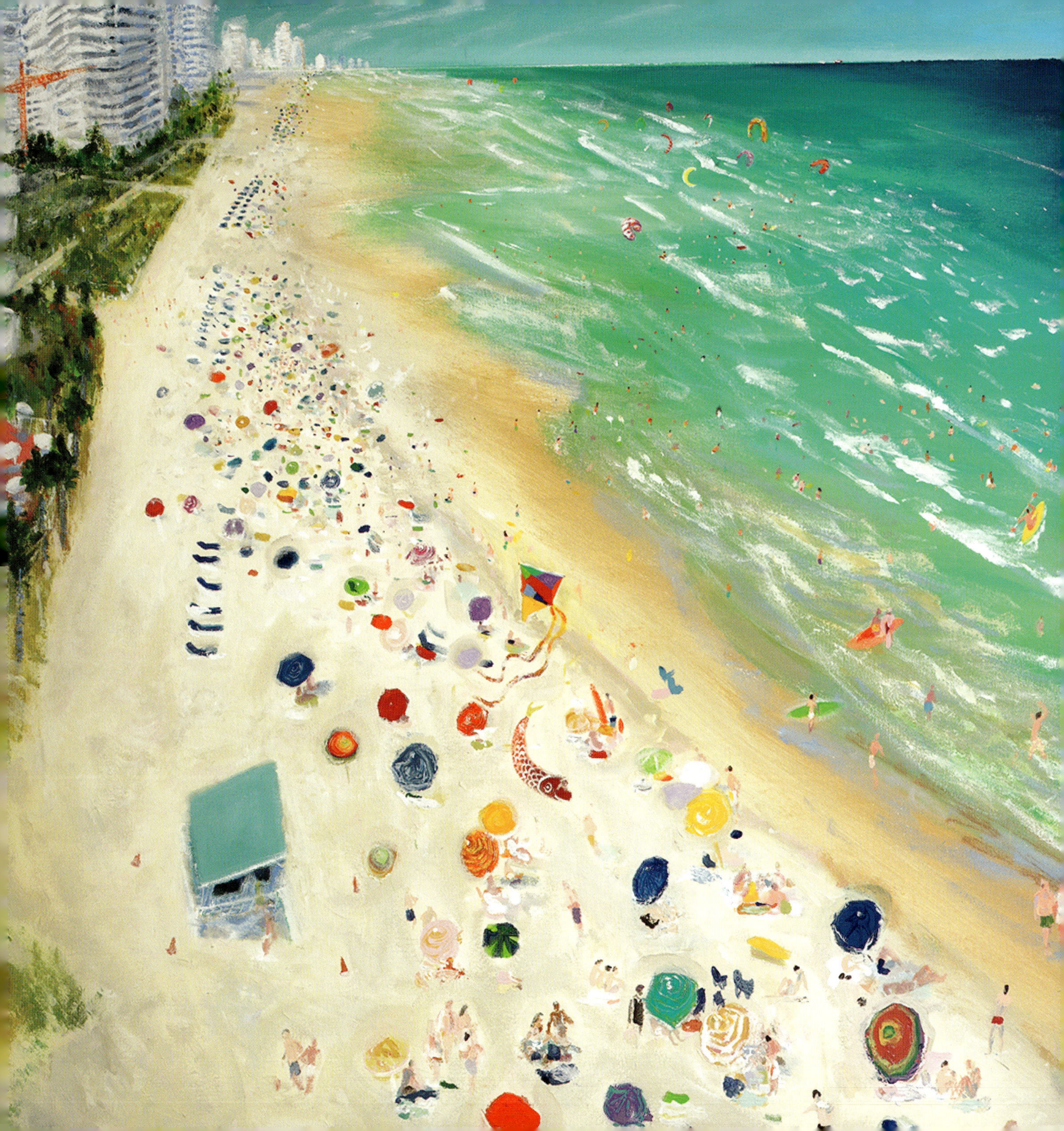

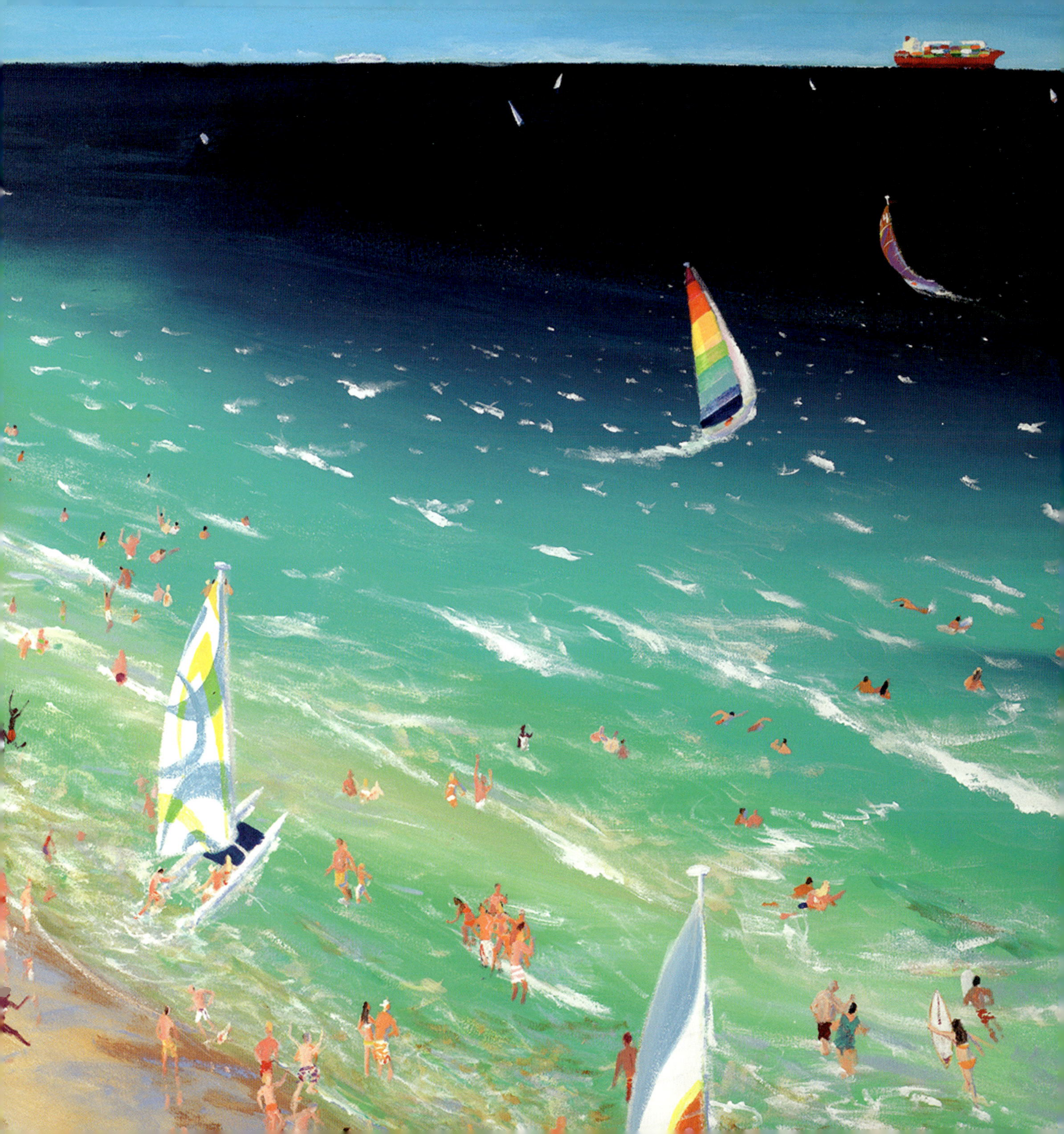

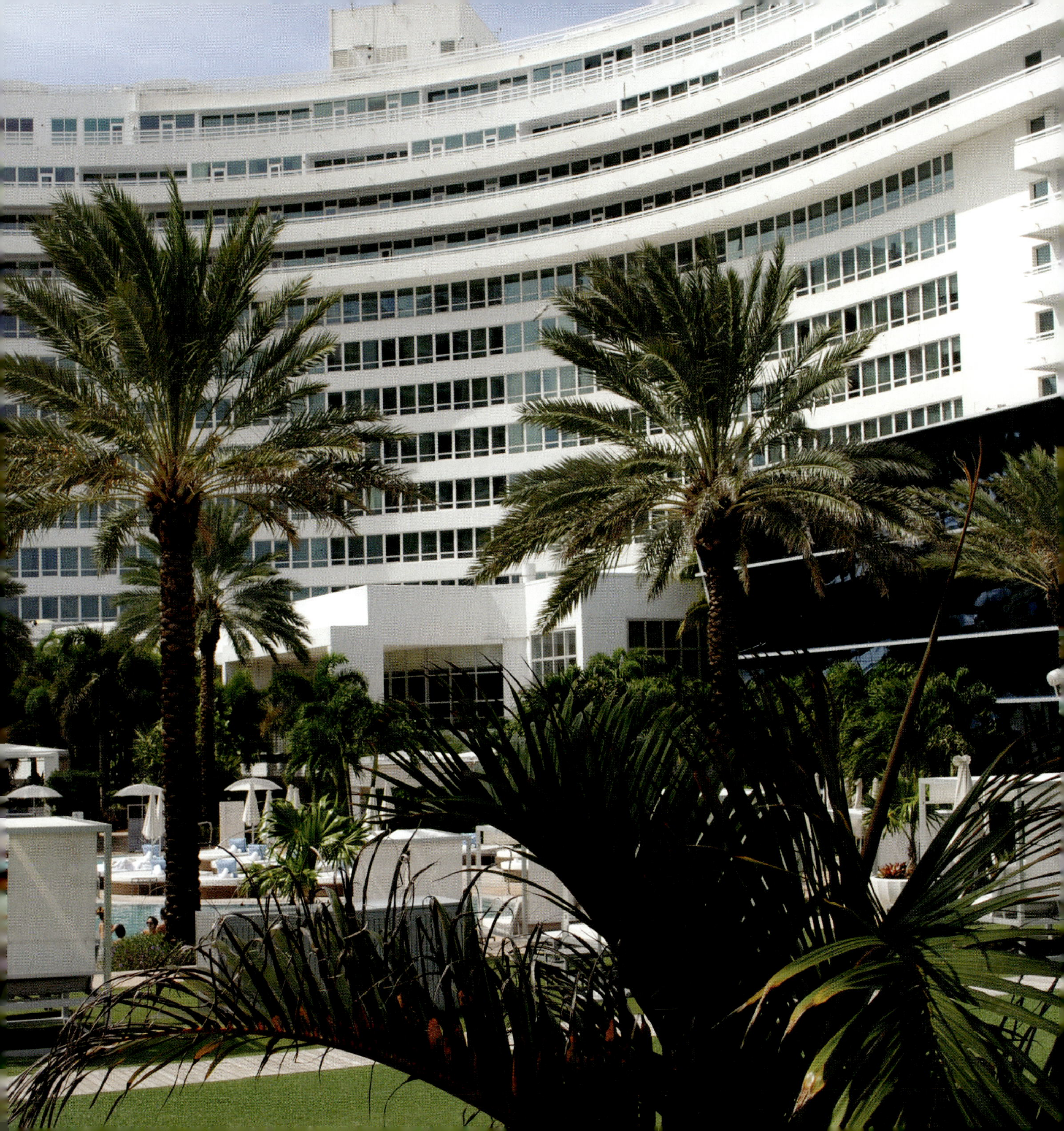

Fontainebleau & Eden Roc Hotels

After World War II, Americans enjoyed a new level of influence and economic prosperity in the world. Many vacationers to Miami Beach were no longer satisfied with small hotel rooms featuring one bathroom per floor which was the standard offering of the older, Art Deco hotels in the southern part of the city. A new generation of modern Miami Beach hotels were created to usher in larger rooms, private bathrooms and greater opportunities to provide entertainment. Developers began scoping out the development potential of the large, gilded estates, remnants of another era, that occupied Miami Beach's "Millionaire's Row" in the mid part of the island city.

The largest and most celebrated of those gilded estates was the Firestone mansion and garden owned by the tire manufacturing magnet Harvey Firestone. After their patriarch's death, the Firestone family entered into quiet negotiations with Ben Novak, a member of a prosperous New York family with resort hotel holdings in the Catskill Mountains and hotel partnerships in several newer resorts in Miami Beach.

The project that Ben Novak had in mind would be his own undertaking, secretly outmaneuvering his Miami Beach partners. The architect that Novack hired to design his groundbreaking resort was relatively unknown, but his impact on Miami Beach architecture would grow to be profound. The elaborate Firestone Estate would give way to architect Morris Lapidus's masterwork. The budget for the hotel was $15 million dollars with only $40,000 allocated for the architect. This was to create dissension between Novack and Lapidus, with Lapidus believing that he was unfairly treated by Novack. The 565 room hotel opened on December 20, 1954. With its now famous dramatically curved lines, cheeseholes, woggles, an elegant lobby featuring bow-tie motif flooring (representing the bow-ties always worn by Novack), and a "floating staircase" the extravagant, glitzy Fontainebleau Hotel captured the imagination of the world.

The interior of the Fontainebleau was a compromise. Owner, Ben Novak, wanted a French Provincial influence, an idea sprung from a recent trip to France with his wife. Architect, Morris Lapidus, an avowed modernist, was horrified by the idea. He presented Novack with an extremely antiquated design rendering of French Provincial furnishings. Novack responded negatively, as Lapidus had hoped. Novak then challenged Lapidus to design "that 'modern' French Provincial". Lapidus proceeded to create a whole new design genre which would evoke strong emotions, pro and con, for decades to come.

The outside of the hotel was such a landmark that it didn't even have a marquee sign until 1977, following an ownership turnover. What it did have and still has, adding to Lapidus' already advanced eclecticism, is a feminine allegorical statue salvaged from the first-class dining salon of the once regal SS Normandie ocean liner.

So glamorous was the new Fontainebleau Hotel that it immediately became a magnet for the leading celebrities of the era; Frank Sinatra, Elvis Presley, Ava Gardner, Dean Martin, Liberace, Red Skelton, Sammy Davis Jr, and later the Bee Gees, and Burt Reynolds. It hosted a slew of movies, among them; The Bellboy (1960), Tony Rome (1967), and most famously, Goldfinger,(James Bond)1968.

The tenuous relationship between Ben Novack and Morris Lapidus finally ruptured in 1955, when Lapidus accepted a commission to design the Eden Roc Hotel, directly neighboring the Fontainebleau. To compound the split, the Eden Roc was a project of Novack's former, now estranged business partner, Harry Mufson. Into the Eden Roc, Lapidus poured his design vision and the epitome of all the glitz he could muster.

An example of the one-upmanship that Lapidus employed at the Eden Roc was to design an even larger "floating staircase" than he had created at the Fontainebleau. The floating staircase provided an entrance from the mezzanine to the lobby. The mezzanine level contained elevators from the upper levels of the hotel. Ladies in their elegant attire would take the elevator to the mezzanine, then descend to the lobby down the staircase to make a grand entrance.

Novack was incensed at the deliberate snubs coming from the Eden Roc. He got his revenge, fourteen years later, when he constructed the North Tower addition to the Fontainebleau. The fourteen story addition blocked out the sun from the swimming pool at the Eden Roc. This became know as the "spite wall".

Novack had a series of bad investments, and eventually lost his hotel on June 28, 1977. In 1978, the Hotelerama Corporation purchased the bankrupt hotel for $27 million dollars and invested an additional $100 million dollars. Eventually the hotel was sold to Turnberry Associates. In 2008, Turnberry Associates launched a $1 billion dollar restoration topping the room count out at 1,504 rooms on 20 oceanfront acres.

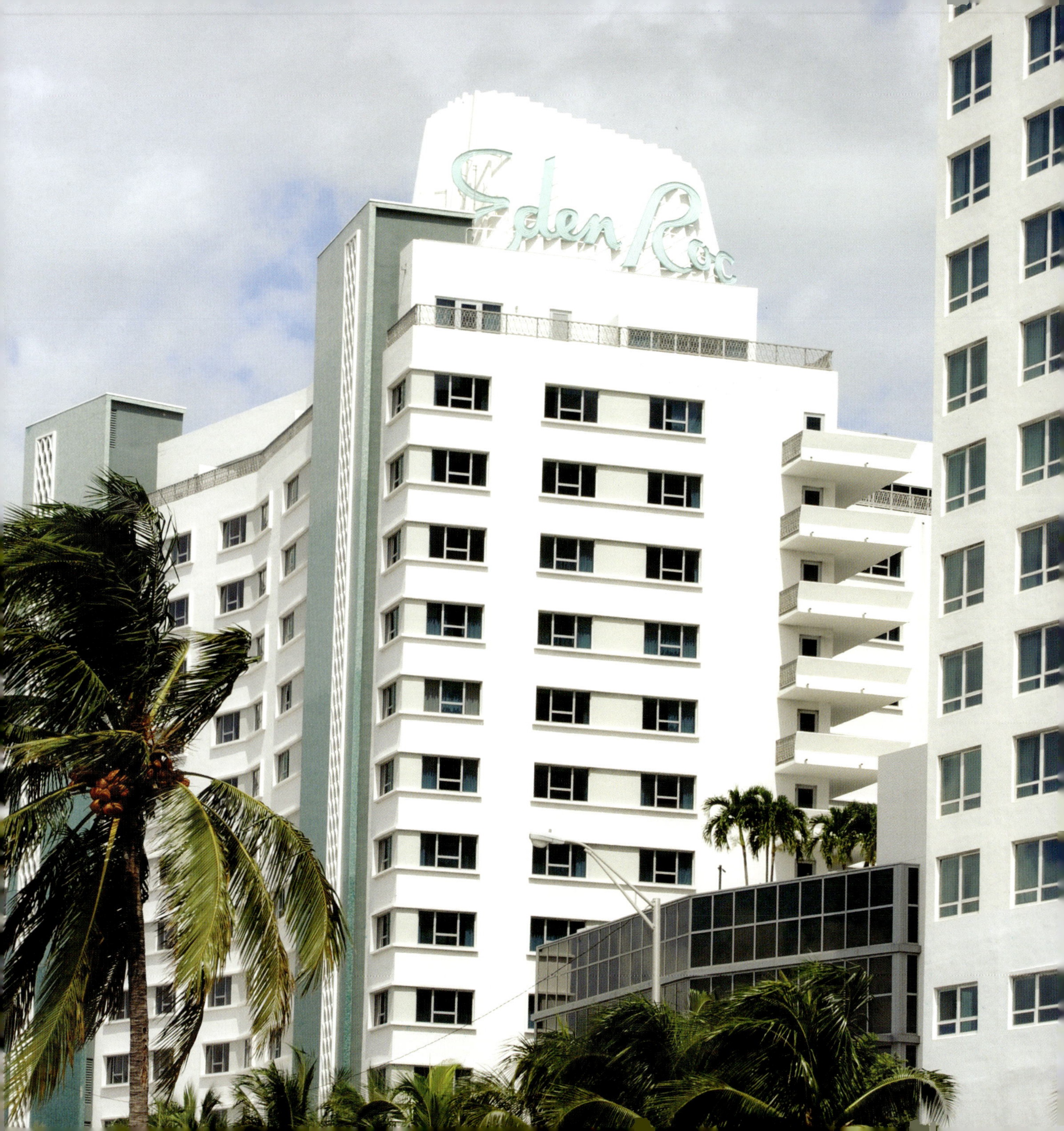
Eden Roc

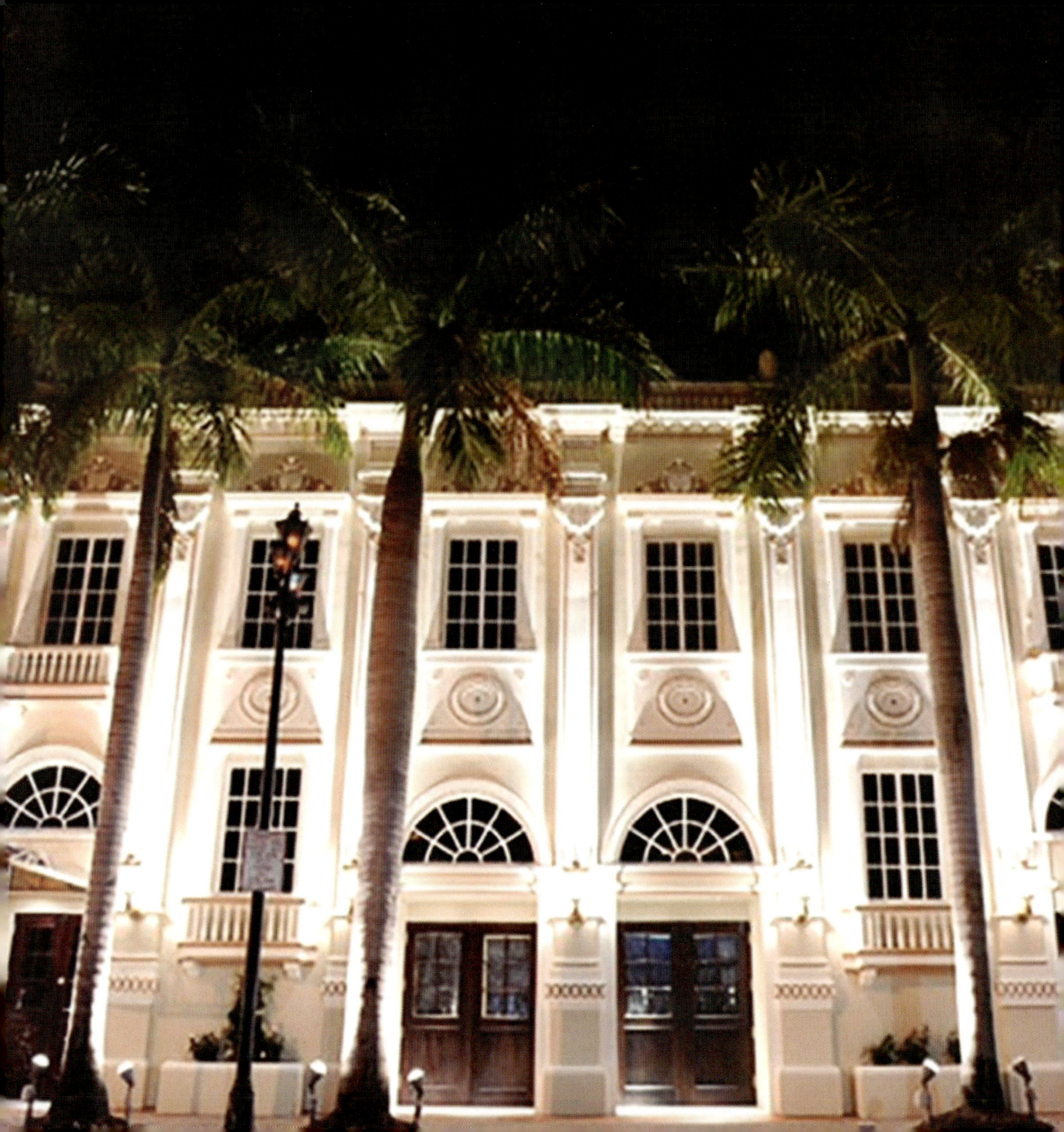

41st Street / Arthur Godfrey Road

Four causeways bring people from mainland Miami to Miami Beach. The MacArthur Causeway, originating in downtown Miami, spills out onto 5th Street in South Beach. The Venetian Causeway brings a more local and subdued traffic pattern into the northern part of South Beach. At the far north, the 79th Street Causeway traverses through Normandy Isles to 71st Street in North Beach. The Julia Tuttle Causeway points traffic directly onto one of Miami Beach's most iconic streets; 41st Street, also known for decades as Arthur Godfrey Road.

Aside from being a local convenience shopping and dining district for Mid Beach, several distinctions make 41st Street stand out. The first is the presence of five synagogues with their schools and facilities representing various denominations of Jewish faith. These synagogues sit directly on 41st Street or one block off of it, providing frequent foot traffic from Orthodox and Hasidic families up and down the thoroughfare.

Another distinction is the presence of a world-famous restaurant called "The Forge", which started its life as an artisan and blacksmith shop in the 1920's, fashioning decorative iron gates and sculptures for Miami Beach's wealthy seasonal residents. In 1939, the owner of the blacksmith shop, Dino Philips, turned the forge into a sophisticated casino and restaurant, drawing such well-known names as Frank Sinatra, Ava Gardner, Judy Garland, Jackie Gleason, Walter Winchell, Arthur Godfrey and Martha Ray.

In 1968, international financier Alvin Malnik purchased the Forge, transformed it into an opulent restaurant and welcomed notables including Richard Burton, Elizabeth Taylor, Desi Arnaz and Richard Nixon. Malnik received a gift of turn-of-the-century wines from Baron Phillippe Rothshild. This kicked off a collection that eventually reached 300,000 vintage bottles in an eight room cellar. One bottle is for sale for $150,000 dollars. When Alvin's son Shareef took over from his father he welcomed celebrities including Michael Jackson, Madonna, Al Pacino, Mikhail Gorbachev and Bill Clinton. Well known criminals also frequented the restaurant throughout the years.

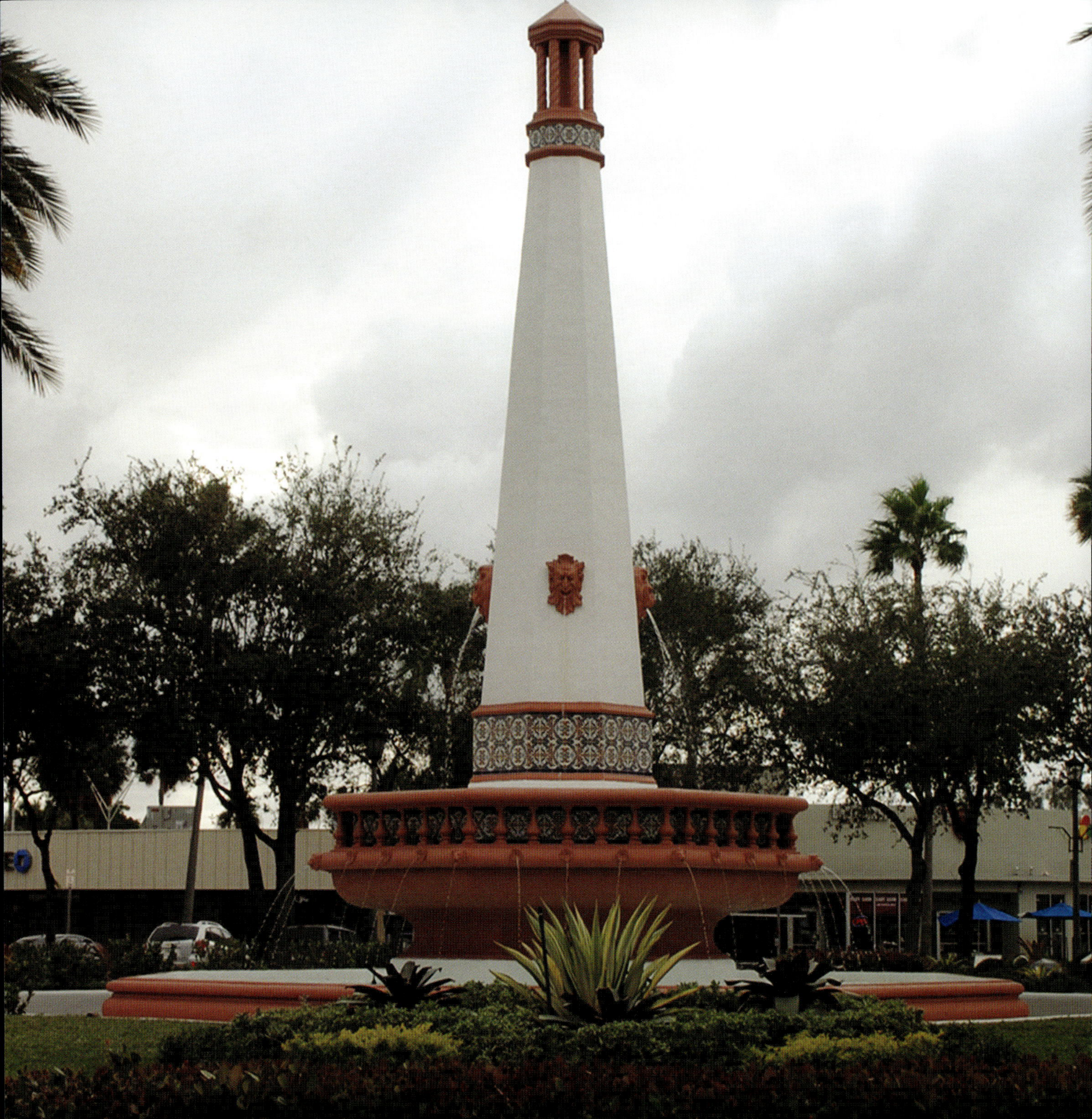

Normandy Isles

Henri Levi, a native of France, became wealthy after creating a chain of theaters in Cincinnati, Ohio. Levi moved to Miami Beach in 1922. He was a friend of Carl Fisher's, even though he was Jewish and Fisher was anti-semitic. It was Fisher's general policy not to sell land to Jewish people. However, when Levi wanted to buy land in Miami Beach, Fisher was willing to sell it to him, but far away from property that he was developing in the southern part of Miami Beach. The land that Levi purchased was in north Miami Beach. Part of that land was in Biscayne Bay and was mostly under water. It was a mangrove patch. Levi convinced some of his associates to invest a quarter of a million dollars to create an island suitable for development. It took two years of dredging, with crews working seven days a week, 24 hours a day, and Normandy Isles was born.

Normandy Isles actually consists of two islands separated by a waterway. The waterway is navigable and connects to Biscayne Bay.

In recognition of Levi's French heritage most of the streets on this man made island were given French names. The island was meant to be luxurious, with a golf course and the water as predominant features. About 80 acres, consisting of about 14 blocks, makes up Normandy Isles. In 1925, Levi had a grand fountain built in the center of Vendome Plaza that welcomes people.

Levi collaborated with government agencies to build a causeway to connect the island to the mainland in 1929. This is the 79th Street Causeway. A number of architects are represented in Normandy Isles and a wide variety of styles exist, including MiMo "Miami Modernism".

Normandy Isles was conceived in the 1920s when the land boom was at its height, so the lots were relatively small, about 50 feet each.

In 2008, Normandy Isles was listed on the National Registry of Historic Places, due to the historic nature of about 200 buildings that are considered architecturally significant.

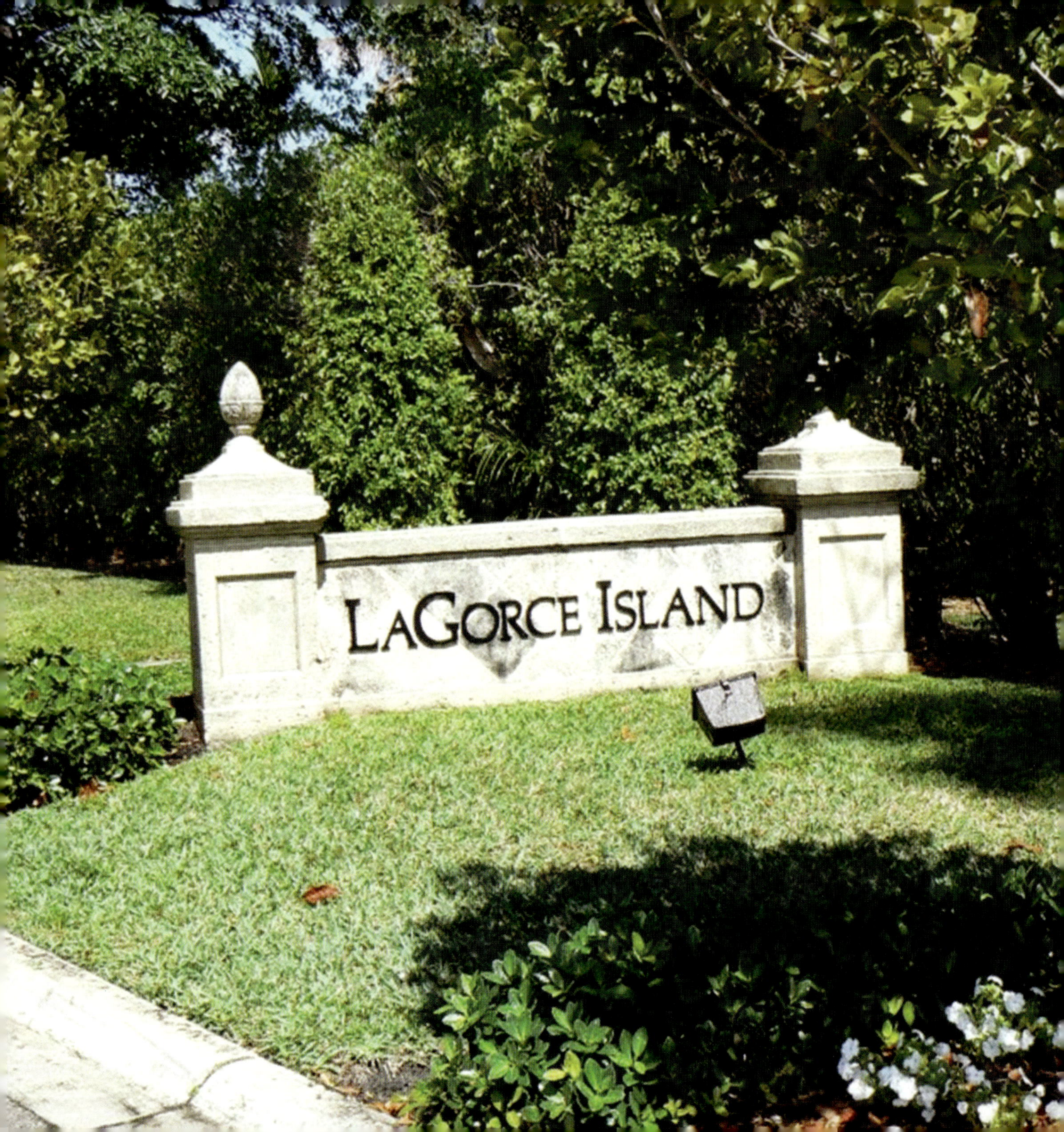
LaGorce Island

LaGorce Island

LaGorce Island, the only private neighborhood in Miami Beach, is an enclave of wealth and privilege in the city. Built in 1924 by the Miami Beach Shore Company, owned by Carl Fisher, the island was named by Fisher for his friend, Dr. John Oliver La Gorce, who was an editor of National Geographic Magazine for fifty years and President for three. He was a well-known Antarctica explorer and adventurer. He shared Fisher's ant-semitic sentiments.

Fisher had more than two million cubic yards of sand dredged from Biscayne Bay to create LaGorce island. Early residents included industrialists John Jacob Astor, Harvey Firestone and the Hertz and Maytag families. Fisher built an exclusive golf club on the island which catered to wealthy families from all over the world and still exists today.

Fisher corresponded with LaGorce and shared his dreams of creating a haven for the wealthy on this island. He wrote of his desire to buy gondolas to ply the waters run by Bahamian natives. LaGorce wrote an article extolling the virtues of this wonderful place. As appreciation, Fisher presented LaGorce with an automobile. While Fisher would not allow Jewish people to join his exclusive club, today it does and even welcomes celebrations of Bar /Bat Mitzvahs and weddings for Jewish people.

LaGorce, using the reach and power of his magazine, (The National Geographic) played an important role in promoting the west side of Miami Beach to the rich and famous. He referred to Miami Beach as a "place for pleasure-bent and health-seeking folk." LaGorce catered to that ideal by offering large lots (some larger than as 20,000 square feet) for waterfront mansions. The island includes 94 residences secured by guards and a private marine patrol.

Many of the mansions on LaGorce Island were designed by distinguished architects of the 1930's and 1940's. In recent years there have been a significant number of tear-downs with the original mansions being replaced by new mega-mansions. Among the famous people who have homes on LaGorce are Cher and Billy Joel.

The island's landscaping features 386 Royal Palms and 775 Silver Date Palms lining the roads.

North Beach

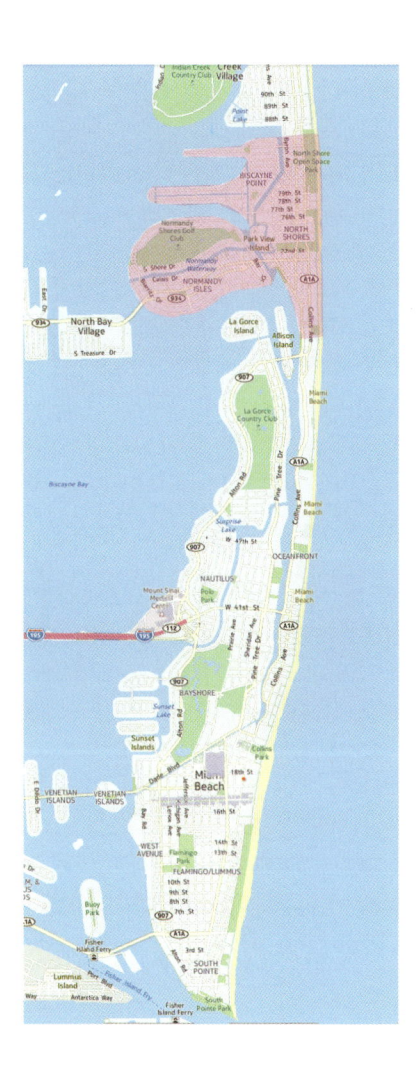

Little Buenos Aires

Mid Century Modern Architecture (MIMO)

North Shore Open Space Park

The North Beach section of Miami Beach running from 63rd Street to 87th terrace has the distinction of being the first place to have a constructed dwelling on Miami Beach, the Biscayne House of Refuge, built in 1876, and the last area of Miami Beach to be fully settled. The House of refuge was built by he U.S. government to provide shelter for people who were shipwrecked and in need of assistance.

Although developers such as Carl Fisher and Henri Levi tried to bring the area to life in the 1920's, it wasn't until the 1950's onward that significant populations began to live in North Beach. This development era coincided with the intense popularity of what is known as MiMo, Miami Modern Architecture.

Today, North Beach with its distinctive architecture, thriving Little Buenos Aires neighborhood, beautiful North Shore Open Space Park and quaint Normandy Isles community, is the focus of renewed redevelopment efforts by the City of Miami Beach and is in the crosshairs of location-hungry developers.

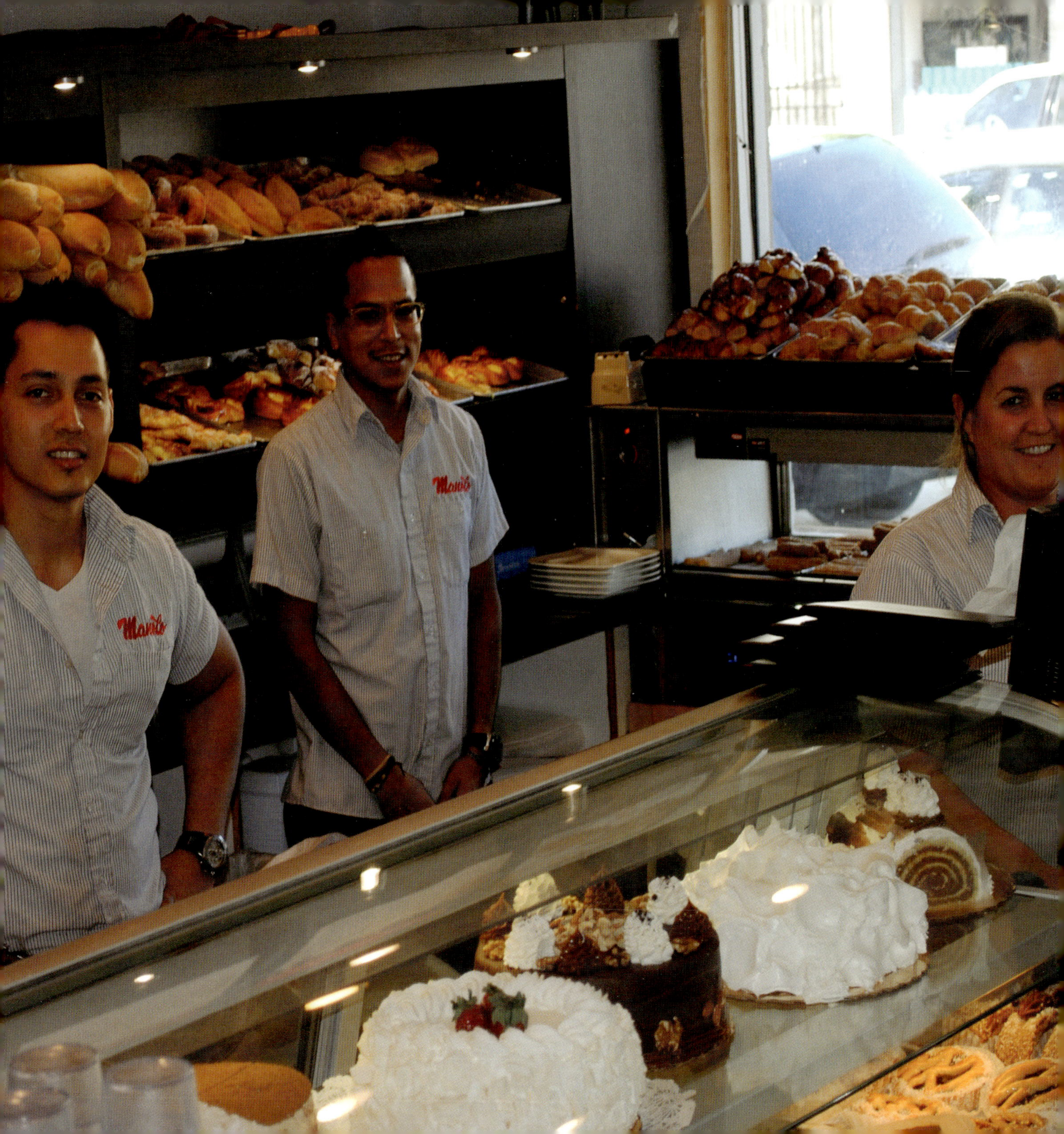

Little Buenos Aires

Throughout the one hundred year history of Miami Beach many waves of people have settled-in and called the City their own. The greater Miami area, including Miami Beach, has a Latin majority. Although most of Miami Beach's Latin population is mixed amongst dozens of Spanish-speaking groups, one group stands out in a large enough aggregation to imprint its name on an entire neighborhood. They are the Argentines and their 10-block enclave is called Little Buenos Aires. Only Little Havana and Little Haiti in the Greater Miami area are concentrated enough to earn similar designations.

The 10-block radius surrounding 71st Street and Collins Avenue encompasses Little Buenos Aires. Here, Argentine restaurants, bars, bakeries and retail shops congregate to serve more than 100,000 expatriates that have settled in the Miami area. Many of these immigrants live in nearby apartments, including classic MiMo garden apartments, and in the Normandy Isles neighborhoods of North Beach. They largely represent working class and middle class Argentine families with their wealthier compatriots choosing such up-market areas as Aventura, Brickell and Key Biscayne. Thousands are in the United States illegally. The unfortunate plight of many of them accelerated in 1999 with the financial meltdown of the Argentine economy. Sovereign default coupled with street protests, economic stagnation, unemployment and increasing crime rates drove many Argentines out of their country. The entrance into the U..S was easy because Argentines were not required to have visas at that time.

As Argentina continued to experience further waves of economic tumult, new groups followed those who arrived in the period between the years of 1999 and 2002. 2014 proved to be difficult in Argentina and a new wave headed to the U.S.

Two important businesses which reflect the Argentine culture are Manolo Restaurant and Buenos Aires Bakery and Cafe. These local institutions keep a busy daily pace, made even busier during soccer matches and championships featuring Argentine teams as well as days of national celebration.

Argentine Spanish has a pronounced tonal differentiation from other spoken forms of Spanish. That accent has grown increasingly familiar to residents and visitors to the North Beach section of Miami Beach.

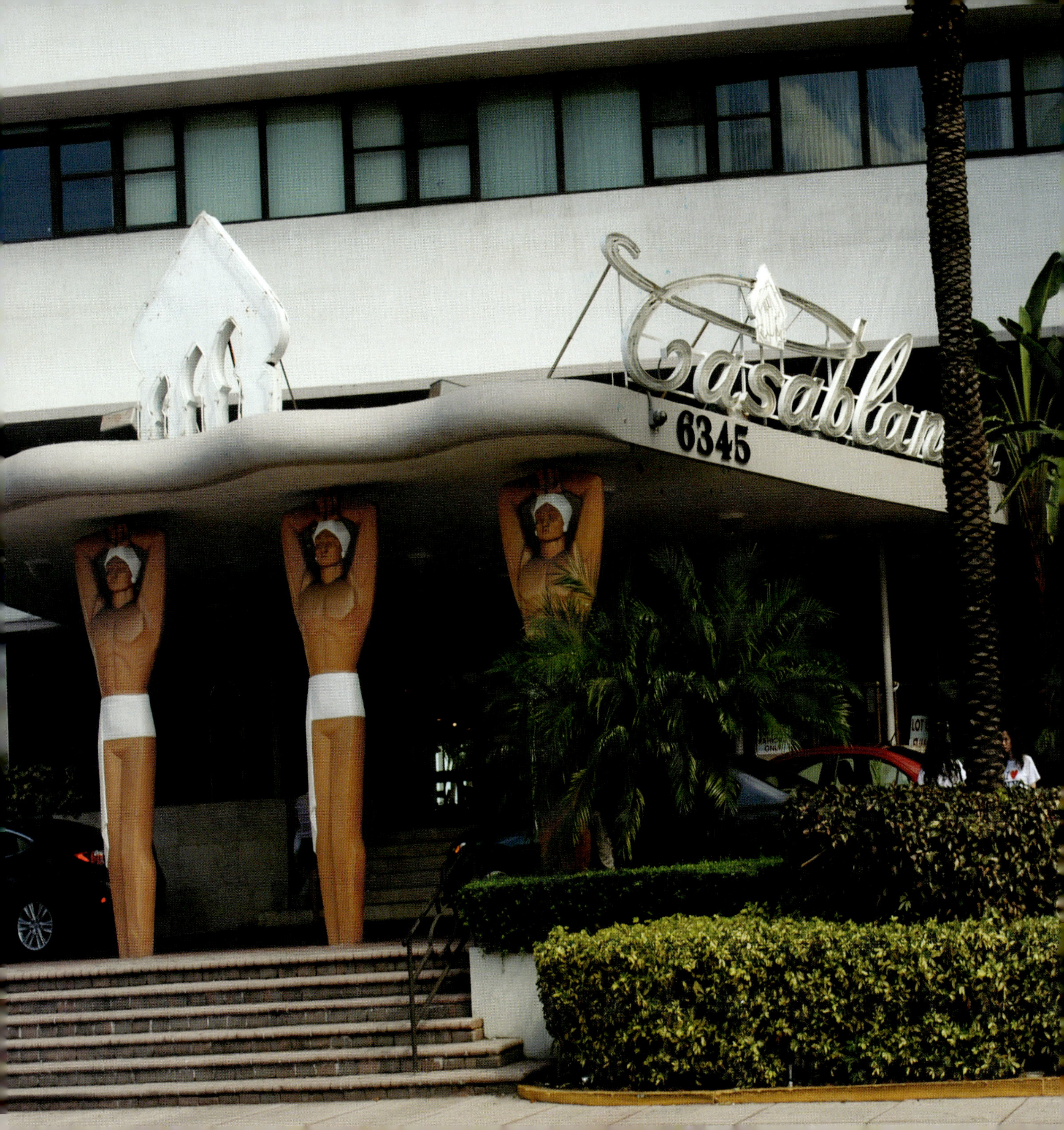
Casablan
6345

MiMo-Miami Modern Architecture

When the idea of preserving an architectural genre begins to take hold, it usually inspires a name. So it was for the style known as Art Deco. Coined in the mid-1960's and popularized by Barbara Capitman in the mid-1970's into the 1980's, Art Deco describes a pre-war modernist style that dominated Miami Beach for decades.

In keeping with this precedent, local preservationist and author Randall C. Robinson, Jr. and Teri D'Amico, an interior designer, coined the phrase "MiMo" to denote Miami's post-war modern architecture. This style came to define Miami Beach in the 1950's and 1960's. Glamorous and distinctive, MiMo is a mix of exuberant modernism, exoticism and thematic playfulness.

MiMo draws from the Bauhaus movement of early 20th century Germany. Bauhaus architects worked around the idea of streamlined, non-ornamental buildings that were comfortable and functional. MiMo took the Bauhaus concept and injected glamour and glitz to the maximum. The extravagant use of glass, aluminum and pre-formed concrete was geometrically sculpted into soaring angles, oval and kidney bean shapes, cantilevered curves and cheeseholes mixed with an inviting kowtow to the American automobile to become the signature of Miami Beach excess.

The leading architects of MiMo; Morris Lapidus, Norman Giller, Igor Polevtsky, Kenneth Treister and Gilbert Fein, among many, were not beyond controversy, receiving scathing and often dismissive reviews from the leading architectural critics of the time. But their "architecture of emotion" as Lapidus described it was suited for the prosperous and exuberant era that it enshrined.

The most renowned examples of MiMo are the Fountainbleau and Eden Roc Hotels. Many beautiful MiMo buildings are currently poised somewhere between the wrecking ball and the prospect of restoration. These include the International Inn, The Deauville, the Casablanca and hundreds of garden apartments and private homes.

Although a vigorous preservationist movement has sprung up, there are crucial obstacles to overcome. Foremost is the current prominent location of many of these buildings in Mid and North Beach where zoning laws allow for greater density, making the buildings a target for developers looking to build new, taller condominiums and larger luxury hotels.

Controversy reigns. There is a growing appreciation for the MiMo architectural style, but there are also many people who do not see the desirability of preserving post-war modernist buildings.

NORTH SHORE OPEN SPACE PARK

North Shore Open Space Park

One of the great treasures of the North Shore sector of Miami Beach is a nine-block long, beach-facing, city-owned public park with plenty of pathways, both paved and unpaved, and an abundance of green space and picnicking locations. The North Shore Open Space Park offers walking, skating and biking paths as well as a separate, fenced-in dog park. Amidst a forest of sheltering native Sea Grape trees, one can find picnic benches, shelters, children's play areas, workout stations and restroom/shower facilities. All of the park's trails lead to a series of paths and boardwalks that traverse the sand dune swales leading out to a wide, panoramic, white sand beach. The Park starts at 78th Street and ends at 87th Terrace. The existence of the park harkens back to the very first structure ever built in what is now the City of Miami Beach. In 1876, by Executive Order from President Ulysses S. Grant, the U.S. Life Saving Service constructed the Biscayne House of Refuge on this stretch of the beach. This was one of a series of such buildings that were built to shelter ship-wrecked sailors and passengers along Florida's long, deserted coast. The House of Refuge was to be SEMPER PARATUS, (always ready). Whenever there was a storm, the keeper and his family were immediately sent out to look for castaways and provide them with food and shelter.

The legendary structure, made of wood and featuring wide, wrap-around porches overlooking the ocean, was a place of gathering for early Miami pioneers. The main floor of the building contained three rooms and a kitchen. On the second floor there was a large dormitory. There were often visitors who stayed for several days, so that it became a small hotel and might be considered the first hostelry on Miami Beach.

It remained intact from 1876 until 1926, when it was destroyed by the Great Hurricane of 1926. It was never rebuilt because better navigation equipment and the development of Miami Beach and the diminishment of wilderness made shipwrecks less frequent. Meanwhile, in 1915, the U.S. Life Saving Service merged with the U.S. Revenue Cutter Service to create the modern-day U.S. Coast Guard. In 1941, when the U.S. Coast Guard moved its facilities to a spoil island off of the MacArthur Causeway, within the southern boundaries of Miami Beach, they conveyed their considerable North Shore holdings to the City of Miami Beach for a public park. Part of the transfer conditions was a mandate that nothing commercial could ever be built on the site. This gift to Miami Beach includes today's North Shore Open Space Park.

Sunset at South Pointe

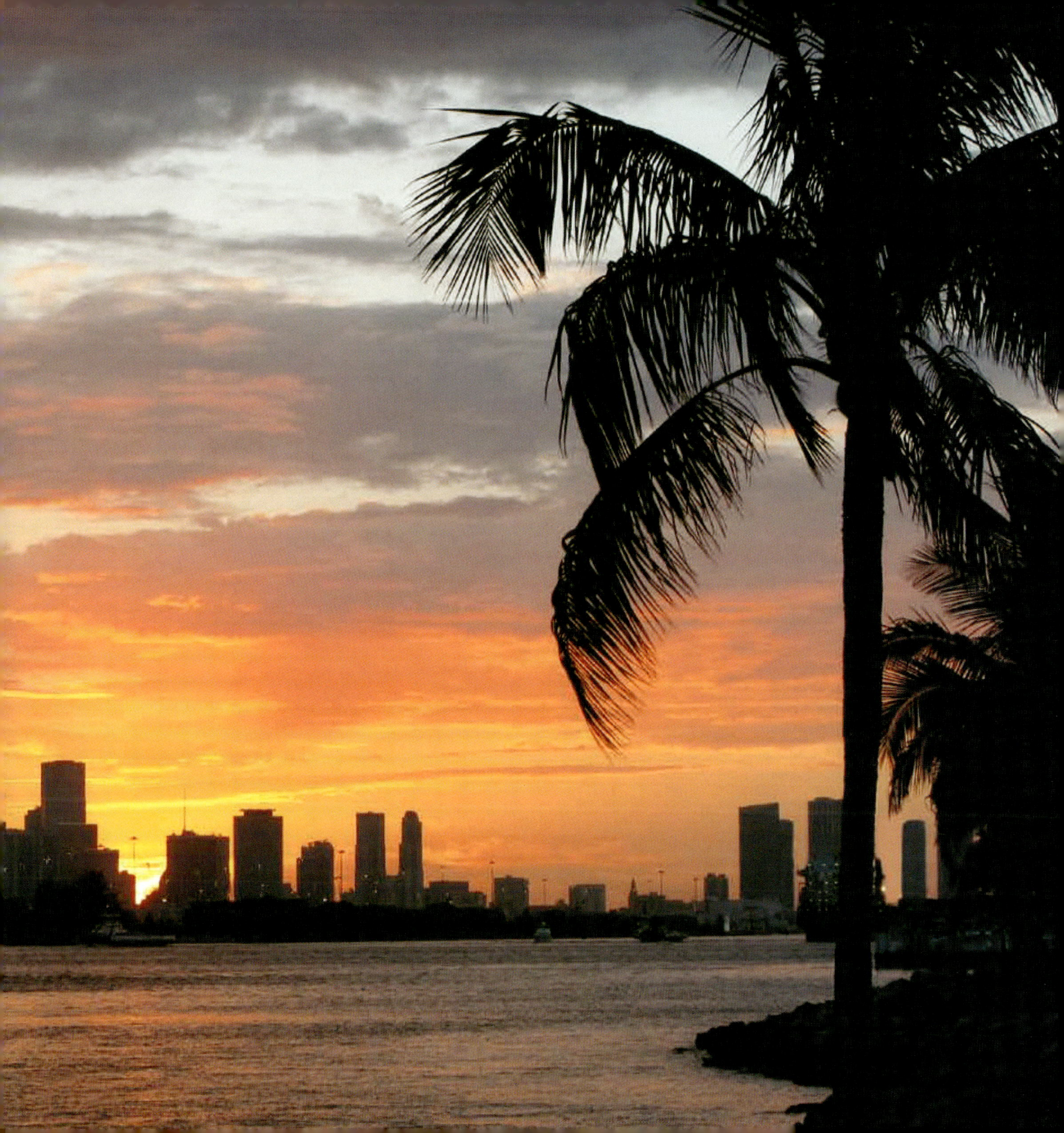

Interviews

Conducted by Charles J. Kropke

Andreano, Vince, Former Chief of the Miami Beach Ocean Rescue Division
Blumberg, Stuart, Former Executive Director of the Miami Beach Convention Center
Bower, Mattie, Mayor of Miami Beach
Carruthers, Cecilia, General Manager of the Clay Hotel
Cary, William, Planner, City of Miami Beach
Doaud, Alex, Former Mayor of Miami Beach and Author
Gardiner, Pamela, Former Executive Director Miami City Ballet
Grafton, Thorn, Architect, Director of Sustainable Initiatives, Great great grandson of John Collins
Gross, Sol, CEO of Streamline Properties
Heisenbottle, Richard, Restoration Architect
Jules, Gary Sanon, General Manager for Tap Tap Restaurant
Kean, Katherine, Owner of Tap Tap Restaurant
Leff, Cathy, Executive Director of Wolfsonian-FIU
Liebman, Nancy, Community Activist
Malnik, Shareef, Owner of The Forge Restaurant
Neary, George, Director of Cultural Tourism, Great Miami Convention and Visitor's Bureau
Parks, Arva Moore, Historian, Author
Robins, Craig, CEO of Dacra Development
Roden, Bryn, Former resident of Amsterdam Palace, (Casa Casuarina)
Sawitz, Steve, Co-owner of Joe's Stone Crab and Great Great Grandson of Joe Weiss
Schlesser, Mel, CEO of Jameck Development
Shulman Allan, Restoration Architect
Soyka, Mark, Owner of the Soyka Group
Tackett, Deborah, Planner, City of Miami Beach
Tisch, Jonathan, CEO of the Loews Corporation
Treister, Kenneth, Architect, and Designer of the Holocaust Memorial
Villela, Edward, Founder of the Miami City Ballet
Wallack, David, Owner of Mango's Tropical Cafe
Weiss, G. Barton, Former owner of Casa Casuarina
Wolfson, Micky, Founder of the Wolfsonian-FIU
Zerivitz, Marcia, Founder of the Jewish Museum of Florida

Bibliography

Books

Armbruster, Ann, THE LIFE AND TIMES OF MIAMI BEACH, Alfred A. Knopf, 1995.
Bass, JoAnn and Sax, Richard, EAT AT JOE'S, Bay Books, 1993.
Bramson, Seth, MIAMI BEACH, IMAGES OF AMERICA, Arcadia Publishing, 2005.
Capitman, Barbara Baer, DECO DELIGHTS, E.P. Dutton, 1988.
Congdon-Martin, Douglas, SOUTH BEACH PERSPECTIVES, Schiffer Publishing Ltd, 2007.
Daoud, Alex, SINS OF SOUTH BEACH, Pegasus Publishing House, 2006.
Gaines, Steven, FOOL'S PARADISE, Crown Publishing Group, 2009.
Kleinberg, Howard, WOGGLES AND CHEESE HOLES, The Greater Miami & Beaches Hotel Association, 2005.
Kleinberg, Howard, MIAMI BEACH, Centennial Press, 1994.
Leddick, David, IN THE SPIRIT OF MIAMI BEACH, Assouline, 2006.
Nash, Eric P. and Robinson, MIMO MIAMI MODERN REVEALED, Chronicle Book, 2004
Parks, Arva Moore, MIAMI; THE MAGIC CITY, Community Media, 2008.
Posner, Gerald, MIAMI BABYLON, Simon and Schuster, 2009.
Raley, H. Michael and Polansky, Linda G. and Millas Aristides, J. OLD MIAMI BEACH, a Case Study in Historic Preservation. July, 1976-July 1980.
Russell, Susan, SOUTH BEACH LIFEGUARD STATIONS, Schiffer Publishing, 2008.
Stofik, M. Barron, SAVING SOUTH BEACH, University Press of Florida, 2005.
Wisser, Bill, SOUTH BEACH, AMERICA'S RIVIERA, Arcade Publishing, 1995.

Magazines

Merritt, Mary Lou, SAND IN THEIR SHOES, and THE RENAISSANCE, SOUTH BEACH STYLE, Yesterday in Florida, Winter 2005

Photo Credits

Pier Entrance, History Miami
Smith's Bathing Casino, Florida History
Collin's Bridge, City of Miami Beach
Bathing Beauties, City of Miami Beach
Soldiers, Florida Memory
Barbara Capitman, Tom Hollyman
    Miami Design Preservation League
Government Cut, Joe Davis
Browns Hotel, Joe Davis
Joe's Stone Crab, Joe Davis
Tap Tap, Bay Proby
Jewish Museum, Joe Davis
Ocean Drive, Joe Davis
Casa Casuarina, Barton G. Images
Lummus Park, Joe Davis
Park Central Hotel, Joe Davis
Wolfsonian - FIU, Joe Davis

Mango's Tropical Cafe, Mango's, David Wallack
Beach Patrol, Joe Davis
Clay Hotel, Joe Davis
Venetian Isles, Bay Proby
Convention Center, Convention Center
Loews Hotel, Joe Davis
New World Symphony, Rui-Dias-Aidos
Holocaust Memorial, Joe Davis
Miami City Ballet, Joe Davis
The Forge, Seth Browarnik
Fontainebleau Hotel, Bay Proby
Eden Roc Hotel, Bay Proby
Normandy Isles, Bay Proby
LaGorce Island, Joe Davis
Manolo, Bay Proby
Casablanca Hotel, Bay Proby
North Shore Open Space Park, Bay Proby

Paintings by Joe Davis

South Pointe
Ocean Drive
Espanola Way
Lincoln Road
The Beach

Tropic Moon Media Documentaries

In collaboration with WXEL, Palm Beach, Florida Public Television, **Tropic Moon Media**, has produced documentaries featuring Charles J. Kropke as creator and host with Emmy award winning producers.

Miami Beach: 100 Years of Making Waves

In celebration of Miami Beach's Centennial, the documentary ***Miami Beach: 100 Years of Making Waves***, chronicles the history of Miami Beach from its early days, when settlers discovered the potential of the sandbar located off of the City of Miami and incorporated Miami Beach as a town on March 26, 1915, till the present glory of this remarkable city. Charles J. Kropke, noted adventure author and tour guide takes the viewer on an unforgettable journey, through present Miami Beach, artfully weaving in its history as he takes them to iconic locations.

The Unseen Everglades: A Legendary Wilderness

In appreciation of the most unusual and diverse ecosystem in the United States, the documentary, ***The Unseen Everglades: A Legendary Wilderness***, tells the story of this national treasure displaying never-before seen locations as Charles J. Kropke takes the viewer from the head-waters of the River at Shingle Creek, to its final destination at Cape Sabal on Florida Bay. The views of the Everglades are spectacular and the astounding history unfolds as Charles interviews experts on every issue confronting this unusual territory.

For information regarding these documentaries available on DVD contact:
Tropic Moon Media
www.tropicmoonmedia.com

Biographies

Charles J. Kropke – Adventurer, Author, Entrepreneur
As managing partner of Dragonfly Expeditions, a 23-year-old travel company of Florida and the Caribbean Basin, Charles has created 150 tours in disciplines such as history, ecology, adventure, and culture, employing over 100 tour guides. In 2013, he received the Outstanding Individual Award from the Dade Heritage Trust. His award-winning book, entitled **SOUTH BEACH**: **Stories of a Renaissance** was chosen by Miami Design Preservation League (MDPL) as book of the year in 2012. Charles has appeared on The Weather and Travel Channels, as well as Russian and German Travel Channels. He is host of a PBS documentary entitled, **THE UNSEEN EVERGLADES**: **Inside A Legendary Wilderness**, in collaboration with WXEL, Palm Beach, FL public television. **MIAMI BEACH: 100 Years of Making Waves**, is accompanied by a documentary, also produced by WXEL.

Eleanor Goldstein – Educator, Author, Publisher
Eleanor is founder of SIRS, Social Issues Resources Series, a company which created exemplary databases utilized in over 60,000 schools and libraries worldwide. She is the author of groundbreaking books on False Memory, three textbooks about Government, Economics and World Affairs. She produced a series of videos bringing together the Florida Philharmonic and the Royal Philharmonic Orchestra of London. She has collaborated with The National Archives, the Library of Congress and the book division of U.S. News & World Report on special projects. Eleanor is co-author with Charles on books and documentaries about Miami Beach and The Everglades.

Joe Davis – Artist, Photographer
During his 15 years in New York City, Joe has had frequent shows, was an Illustrator for The New Yorker Magazine and The New York Times Sunday Magazine. He recently concentrates on beach scenes of Florida which are collector's items.

Charles    **Eleanor**    **Joe**

Contact Information

TROPIC MOON MEDIA
A documentary film making and publishing company.

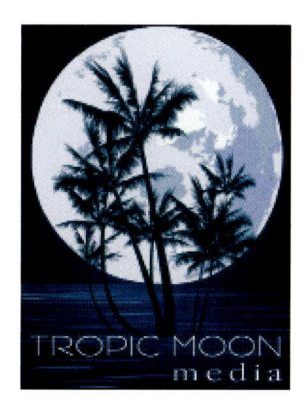

www.tropicmoonmedia.com

Published by
Interactive Learning and Technology
dba
Tropic Moon Media
1100 Holland Drive, Boca Raton, Florida 33487

ISBN 978-1-4951-4480-6

© 2015 by Eleanor Goldstein, Publisher

No part of this book may be reproduced in any manner or transmitted by any means whatsoever, electronic or mechanical (including photocopy, recording, internet posting or any other information storage and retrieval system), without the prior written permission of the publisher.